Do-it-Yourself
BASICS

··

Save Money • Solve Problems • Improve Your Home

THE BASICS EVERYONE CAN MASTER

Reader's
Digest

New York, NY/Montreal

Do-It-Yourself Basics

Content Management Mary Flanagan
Design Elizabeth Tunnicliffe
Page Layout David Farr
Proofreader Judy Arginteanu

Text, photography and illustrations for *Do-It-Yourself Basics* are based on articles previously published in *Family Handyman* magazine (2915 Commers Dr., Suite 700, Eagan, MN 55121, familyhandyman.com). For information on advertising in *Family Handyman* magazine, call (646) 518-4215.

Family Handyman ISBN: 978-1-62145-500-4 (dated)
Family Handyman ISBN: 978-1-62145-501-1 (undated)
Reader's Digest ISBN: 978-1-62145-505-9

Front cover, large photo: Sirtravelalot/Shutterstock.com
Back cover, large photo: InkDrop/Shutterstock.com

Address any comments to:
feedback@familyhandyman.com

A Note to Our Readers

All do-it-yourself activities involve a degree of risk. Skills, materials, tools and site conditions vary widely. Although the editors have made every effort to ensure accuracy, the reader remains responsible for the selection and use of tools, materials and methods. Always obey local codes and laws, follow manufacturer instructions and observe safety precautions.

Pricing

Professional services and supplies can vary widely depending on the market. Those listed are average costs and are just a guide to cost savings.

The Family Handyman

EDITORIAL
Chief Content Officer Nick Grzechowiak
Editor-in-Chief Gary Wentz
Managing Editor Donna Bierbach
Assigning Editor Berit Thorkelson
Associate Assigning Editor Mary Flanagan
Associate Editors Mike Berner, Jay Cork, Brad Holden, Jason Ingolfsland
Contributing Copy Editor Peggy Parker
Contributing Editors Spike Carlsen, Rick Muscoplat
Lead Carpenter Josh Risberg
Editorial Services Associate Peggy McDermott

ART
Associate Creative Director Vern Johnson
Graphic Designer Mariah Cates
Photographer Tom Fenenga

Trusted Media Brands, Inc.
President & Chief Executive Officer
Bonnie Kintzer

PRINTED IN CHINA

1 2 3 4 5 6 7 8 9 10

Safety first—always!

Tackling home improvement projects and repairs can be endlessly rewarding.
But as most of us know, with the rewards come risks.
The good news is, armed with the right knowledge, tools and procedures, homeowners
can minimize risk. As you go about your projects and repairs, stay alert for these hazards:

Aluminum wiring

Aluminum wiring, installed in about 7 million homes between 1965 and 1973, requires special techniques and materials to make safe connections. This wiring is dull gray, not the dull orange characteristic of copper. Hire a licensed electrician certified to work with it. For more information go to cpsc.gov and search for "aluminum wiring."

Spontaneous combustion

Rags saturated with oil finishes like Danish oil and linseed oil, and oil-based paints and stains can spontaneously combust if left bunched up. Always dry them outdoors, spread out loosely. When the oil has thoroughly dried, you can safely throw them in the trash.

Vision and hearing protection

Safety glasses or goggles should be worn whenever you're working on DIY projects that involve chemicals, dust and anything that could shatter or chip off and hit your eye. Sounds louder than 80 decibels (dB) are considered potentially dangerous. Sound levels from a lawn mower can be 90 dB, and shop tools and chain saws can be 90 to 100 dB.

Lead paint

If your home was built before 1979, it may contain lead paint, which is a serious health hazard, especially for children 6 and under. Take precautions when you scrape or remove it. Contact your public health department for detailed safety information or call (800) 424-LEAD (5323) to receive an information pamphlet. Or visit epa.gov/lead.

Smoke and carbon monoxide (CO) alarms

The risk of dying in reported home structure fires is cut in half in homes with working smoke alarms. Test your smoke alarms every month, replace batteries as necessary and replace units that are more than 10 years old. As you make your home more energy-efficient and airtight, existing ducts and chimneys can't always successfully vent combustion gases, including potentially deadly carbon monoxide (CO). Install a UL-listed CO detector, and test your CO and smoke alarms at the same time.

Five-gallon buckets and window covering cords

From 1996 to 1999, 58 children under age 5 drowned in 5-gallon buckets. Always store them upside down and store ones containing liquid with the covers securely snapped.

According to Parents for Window Blind Safety, 599 children have been seriously injured or killed in the United States since 1986 after becoming entangled in looped window treatment cords. For more information, visit pfwbs.org or cpsc.gov.

Working up high

If you have to get up on your roof to do a repair or installation, always install roof brackets and wear a roof harness. If you have to work on a ladder on the second story or higher, remember the three points of contact rule: Always have two hands and one foot or two feet and one hand on the ladder.

Asbestos

Texture sprayed on ceilings before 1978, adhesives and tiles for vinyl and asphalt floors before 1980, and vermiculite insulation (with gray granules) all may contain asbestos. Other building materials, made between 1940 and 1980, could also contain asbestos. If you suspect that materials you're removing or working around contain asbestos, contact your health department or visit epa.gov/asbestos for information.

Buried utilities

A few days before you dig in your yard, have your underground water, gas and electrical lines marked. Just call 811 or go to call811.com.

➤ **For additional information about home safety, visit mysafehome.org.**
This site offers helpful information about dozens of home safety issues.

Contents

Chapter 1 DIY Fundamentals

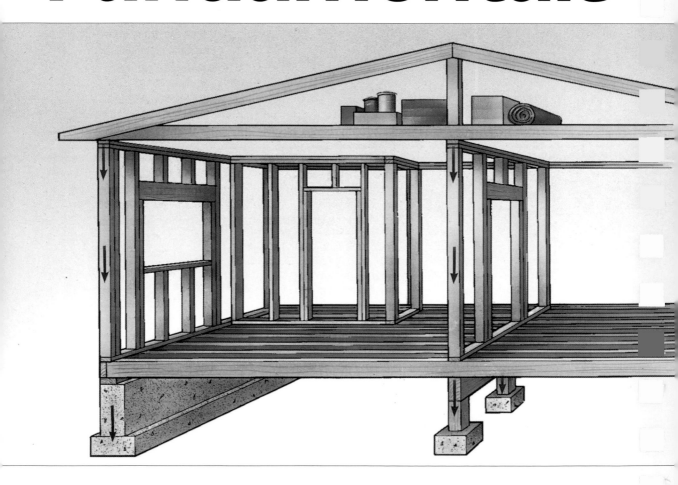

DIY vs. PAP

There are two approaches to home improvement: DIY and PAP. If you're reading this book, you're probably of the DIY (do-it-yourself) persuasion. You roll up your sleeves and tackle the job yourself. You know you can save money, control the schedule, learn new skills and add your own personal touches. Others are PAP (point-and-pay) people. They call the electrician or plumber, point out the problem, and then pay a pro to do the work.

The truth is, most homeowners alternate between these two approaches— and that's just fine. Some feel comfortable with a router but run at the sight of a dripping faucet. Others may feel confident installing a new light fixture but cringe at the thought of hanging a new exterior door.

Regardless of your approach, knowing more about the steps, tools, materials and pitfalls will help your projects go more smoothly. And know-how is what this book is all about.

10 guidelines for successful home improvement

1. **Be realistic.** Most manuals, TV shows and books present projects and repairs in a perfect-world scenario. But we live in an imperfect world where bolts stick and floors aren't level. Things may very well take longer, cost more and use more materials than you expect.

2. **Be safe.** Wear hearing, eye and breathing protection to save yourself from injury and years of misery.

3. **Invest in the best tools you can afford to buy (or rent).** You'll work faster, safer and with more enjoyment.

4. **Know when to stop.** Figure out the logical stopping points and then stop. Most accidents happen when people get tired.

5. **Measure twice, cut once.** You'll save tons of time and material.

6. **Be prepared.** There's no such thing as one trip to the hardware store. Buy extra and return what you don't use. Before you take it apart, take a picture of it.

7. **Remember the big picture.** What you do at point A may affect point B. For example, if you insulate your attic, make certain you don't block the roof vents.

8. **It's OK to ask directions.** Really.

9. **Think like a drop of water.** Water in the wrong place—whether from a broken pipe, condensation or rain—causes more problems than anything else.

10. **Finish the job.** If you don't install that last piece of molding while your tools are out, the project may go unfinished forever.

Planning

Most projects and repairs are done twice: first in your head, with CAD or on paper, next with a wrench or saw in your hand. Don't shortchange the first part of the process. Whether it's ordering the right amount of lumber for your deck or plotting out your bathroom remodeling project so your family isn't without water for three days, planning can make or break a home improvement project. This first step takes a little extra time up front, but in the end you'll experience fewer hassles and more peace of mind.

The best time to gather information, determine a game plan, arrange for outside help and round up your tools and materials is before the dust flies. Think ahead.

Permits

Many home-improvement projects require you, or your contractor, to obtain a permit. Obtaining permits can be a hassle, but getting caught doing work without one, or using substandard building practices, can be much worse.

Frequently required permits

Permit requirements vary greatly from one community to the next. Some common projects requiring permits include:

➤ Projects involving structural alterations to your house, such as adding a larger window or removing a wall.

➤ Installing a deck, fence, outbuilding or pool.

➤ Finishing a basement or attic space.

➤ Adding an electrical branch circuit, outlet or fixture.

➤ Installing or replacing a water heater, furnace, air conditioner or fireplace.

Depending on the project, you may or may not be required to submit a blueprint or plan.

Inspections

Some small projects may require a single inspection, while larger ones may require a dozen or more. Make certain you know when and where inspections are required. Also remember you may not be able to move to the next step of your project until the inspection has been completed. Plan and schedule ahead.

Frequently required inspections

➤ Footing inspections (after the footings are formed, but before the concrete is poured).

➤ Framing inspections (after the framing materials and sheathing are in place).

➤ Rough plumbing/gas line inspection (while pipes are exposed).

➤ Final plumbing inspection (supply and drain/waste/vent pipes are pressure tested for leaks).

➤ Insulation inspection (sometimes after the vapor barrier is installed).

➤ Drywall inspection (often after drywall has been fastened, but before taping begins).

➤ Rough-in electrical inspection (rough wiring completed in electrical boxes but devices such as switches, outlets and light fixtures not installed).

➤ Final electrical inspection (all switches, outlets and lights in place and wiring at circuit panel complete).

➤ Final inspection (final check to make sure all codes have been followed).

Working with contractors

Though stories of unscrupulous contractors abound, most in the business are honest, hardworking folks. Most live and die by their reputations. Those who take the money and run or do substandard work don't stay in business long.

Yet, there are things you should check out.

Questions to ask, things to check

1. Legal matters. Do they have the proper licenses and insurance to work in your community? Ask to see the actual documents.

2. Contract. The more specific, the better. Specify the exact materials to be used, right down to the manufacturer, when necessary.

3. References. Will they provide names and contact information for their most recent clients? If the references are old or few-and-far-between, ask why. How long have they been in business? Check with the Better Business Bureau to see if any complaints have been filed.

4. Down payment and money matters. Determine at what points in the project payments will be made. One-third down for materials is common.

5. Work schedule. What date will the project start and what is a realistic date of completion?

6. Changes. Commonly, a change order spelling out the design and financial implications is drawn up and signed by the homeowner and contractor when there is a change in the initial contract.

7. On the job. Determine to whom you'll speak regarding the day-to-day operations. Who handles questions? How early in the day would work start and how long would it go on in the evening? What about a bathroom, smoking and eating considerations for workers? Who cleans up and when?

How your home is built

Bearing vs. nonbearing walls

There are two kinds of walls in your house—bearing and nonbearing. Bearing walls are exterior and interior walls that transfer the weight of the roof, floors and walls above them down to the foundation. Since these walls carry a lot of weight, studs removed during remodeling must be replaced by a header that transfers the weight over to the sides of the opening, then down to the foundation. Bearing walls usually (but not always) run perpendicular to the floor and ceiling joists. And exterior walls are usually bearing walls if the rafters overlap them. If you check your basement for posts, walls and beams, the interior walls located above them are usually bearing walls. But there are exceptions. Joists and roof members can change directions.

Nonbearing walls need to support themselves, but not much weight from above. Interior nonbearing walls simply divide up space. Nonbearing exterior walls usually run parallel to the roof trusses and floor joists above. But if you create an opening in a nonbearing wall, it's still a good idea to install a substantial header, so the opening doesn't sag under its own weight. When in doubt, consult an inspector.

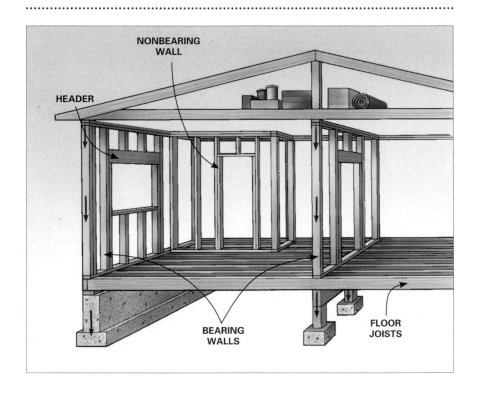

NONBEARING WALL

HEADER

BEARING WALLS

FLOOR JOISTS

Wall bracing

If you've ever carried a sheet of plywood in a strong breeze, you know how strong a force the wind can be. Your house needs to stand up to these same winds, year after year. And occasionally it needs to stand up against the violent forces of a thunderstorm, hurricane or tornado. To withstand all this, your home contains several types of bracing.

Wall bracing, which prevents your walls from going out of plumb, can be in the form of plywood or other sheathing nailed to the studs or in the form of steel or wood cross-bracing notched into, or secured to, the studs. Chances are, if you crawl around in your attic, you'll find other types of diagonal bracing nailed to the trusses or crossties that also help keep your walls straight and strong.

In areas with a threat of earthquakes, many other forms of bracing are required. Suffice it to say, you should not remove braces or parts of braces in the course of remodeling. When in doubt, consult a building inspector.

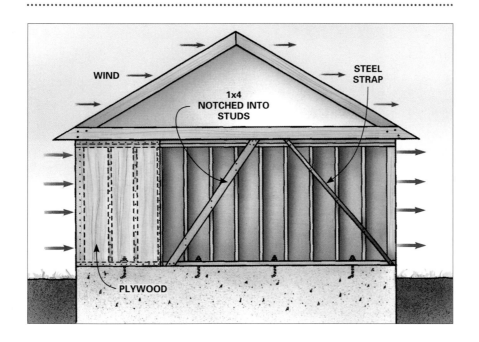

WIND

STEEL STRAP

1x4 NOTCHED INTO STUDS

PLYWOOD

Typical interior wall

Before you pick up a sledgehammer and bash out that wall, think about what's inside. Any given wall can contain electrical wires, gas pipes, hot and cold water lines, drain and vent pipes, heat ducts, cold air return ducts, radiator piping and more. These "surprises" may need to be rerouted and can turn a small project into a big one or, worse yet, a doable project into an impossible one.

As you plan, pay visits to the basement and attic to find out what pipes, wires and ducts enter or leave the wall. Walls around kitchens and bathrooms usually contain the most stuff, while exterior walls, especially in cold climates, usually contain only wires.

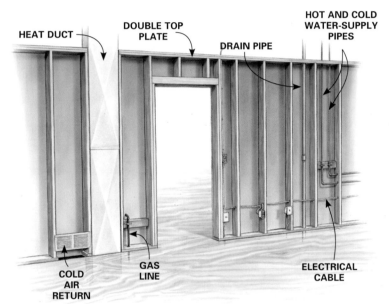

HEAT DUCT

DOUBLE TOP PLATE

DRAIN PIPE

HOT AND COLD WATER-SUPPLY PIPES

COLD AIR RETURN

GAS LINE

ELECTRICAL CABLE

Typical exterior wall

The 2x4 or 2x6 studs and plates that create the framework for an exterior wall do triple duty: They support the roof and floors above; create a cavity for pipes, wires, ductwork and insulation; and provide a flat, uniform surface for applying plywood, drywall and other materials.

On the exterior, most walls are covered with plywood, rigid foam or some other sheathing. Over that, felt paper, house wrap or wind infiltration barrier is often installed. The final layer can be wood, vinyl or steel siding, stucco or brick.

On the interior side, most walls contain insulation and a vapor barrier along with drywall or plaster.

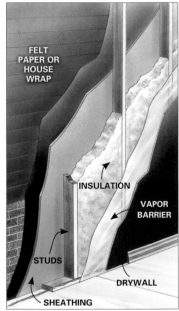

FELT PAPER OR HOUSE WRAP

INSULATION

VAPOR BARRIER

STUDS

DRYWALL

SHEATHING

Basic structure

Our homes rarely let us down because, even as they evolved architecturally, wood frame houses maintained basic design principles that make them sturdy.

Below is a an example. The weight from the roof compresses the rafters and tenses the ceiling joists. These forces transfer the weight to the load-bearing walls. Weight compresses the wood along the top of the floor joists. It also tenses the wood along the bottom, which allows the floor joists to transfer weight to the bearing walls. The foundation transfers weight to the ground.

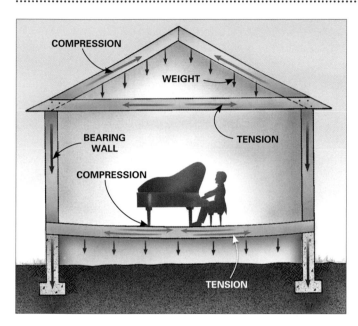

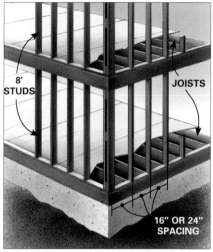

Platform framing is the standard residential construction method used today. It allows builders and do-it-yourselfers to use shorter and lighter framing members than houses of the past. Studs, joists and rafters are typically spaced at 16- or 24-in. intervals to create strength and make optimum use of standard materials such as 2x4 studs, 4x8 sheets of plywood and 4x12 sheets of drywall.

Electrical basics

Working with electricity is neither difficult nor dangerous as long as you understand this powerful phenomenon and treat it with respect. Here you'll learn how your system works and how to assess it, upgrade it, add to it and make repairs. You'll also be able to tell whether a wiring job is within your reach or best left to a licensed electrical contractor.

If you're a beginner, read carefully before attempting any electrical projects. Pay special attention to all safety precautions and learn how to safely use electrical testers and tools.

Just what is electricity? Think of it as a stream of negatively charged particles, called electrons, flowing at 186,000 miles per second (the speed of light) through a conductor, a wire, much the way water flows through a pipe.

The electrical pressure that causes current to flow through a conductor is measured in volts. Light fixtures and small appliances operate on 120 volts, and electric ranges and other heavy-duty appliances require 240 volts.

Resistance to the flow of electrons will vary with different materials. Copper is a good conductor and has low resistance, unlike plastic wire insulation that has very high resistance.

The rate that electric current flows is measured in amperes (amps). One ampere is the amount of current that will flow through one ohm—a measure of resistance-with a pressure of 1 volt.

The amount of power delivered by a current under pressure to a lamp or appliance is measured in watts. Watts, volts and amps are all interrelated. If you know two of the variables, you can figure out the third. You can also determine the cost of running appliances and equipment.

Simple circuits. To do work, electricity must flow in a closed loop or circuit from a power source to a load, such as a lightbulb, then back to the source. If the circuit is interrupted by a switch or blown fuse, the current flow stops.

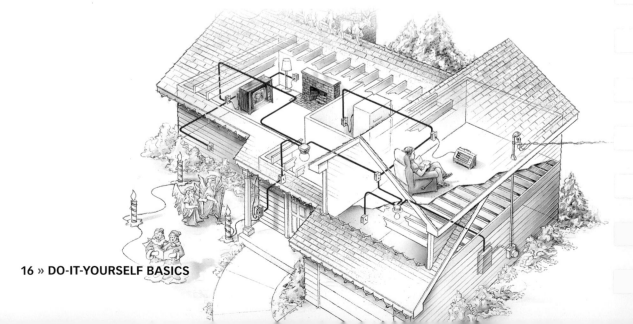

How power reaches your home. The electricity generated by a power plant and delivered to your home by your local utility is called alternating current (AC) because it flows alternately, first in one direction, then in the opposite, completing 60 cycles every second. (Batteries produce direct current (DC) that flows through a circuit in only one direction.) From the power plant, current travels over high-voltage transmission lines to substations, where transformers reduce the voltage for distribution to local lines. Neighborhood transformers lower the voltage to 120 and 240 volts for household use.

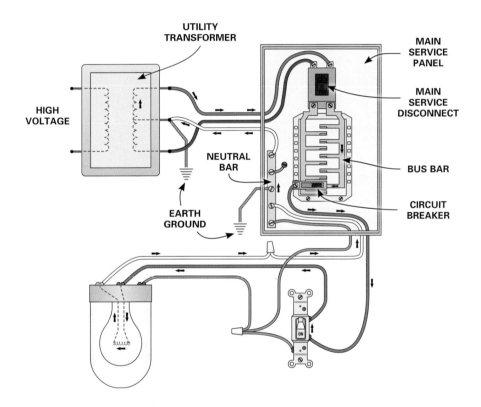

A simple circuit. In a typical lighting circuit, current flows at 120 volts from a common hot bus bar in the main service panel through a hot wire (usually color-coded black) to a lightbulb's wire filament (for incandescent bulbs), where it produces heat and light. From the bulb, a neutral wire (usually color-coded white) completes the circuit path back to the panel's neutral bar, which is grounded (connected to the earth). If a circuit malfunctions, a grounding wire (bare copper or color-coded green), running with the hot and neutral wires, provides a safe path to the source for abnormal current flow. The grounding wire enables overcurrent protective devices, like circuit breakers, to work.

Homes built after the late 1960s will have 100-amp (or larger), 120- and 240-volt, three-wire service. Some homes built in the early 1900s may still have 30-amp, 120-volt, two-wire service. The most common pre-1960s service was three-wire, from 30 to 60 amps.

Electrical service may be supplied through overhead or underground wires. The utility's overhead service drop is connected to the home's service-entrance wires at the weatherproof service head, where they are installed in conduit to the meter enclosure. For underground services, the utility's direct-buried wires run to the home, where they emerge from the ground in a short conduit sleeve and connect inside the electrical meter box.

From the meter enclosure, the service-entrance wires run to the service panel, usually inside the home, where they terminate at the main service disconnect (see illustration on p. 17). The service disconnect is the first overcurrent protective device in the home; therefore, the length of unfused service-entrance wires inside the home must be kept as short as possible. From the service panel, electricity is distributed by branch circuits.

Circuit breakers and fuses

Branch circuits that distribute electricity throughout the house are typically rated from 15 to 50 amps. When a circuit draws too much current, wires can overheat, insulation can degrade and fail and the risk of fire greatly increases. To prevent this, each circuit is protected at the service panel by an overcurrent protective device. Most pre-1965 panels have fuses, and newer panels have circuit breakers. If a circuit draws excess current, the breaker will trip off or the metal strip inside the fuse melts open, stopping current flow.

Circuit failures are often caused by overloads, short circuits and ground faults. **Overloads** are caused when too many lights or appliances are on a circuit. **Short circuits** occur when a hot wire touches the neutral wire or another hot wire. A hot wire that touches a grounded metal box would be a **ground fault**. Before resetting the breaker or

Panels

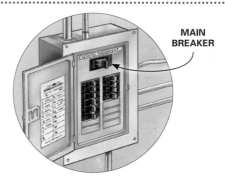

A circuit-breaker panel will usually have a double-pole main breaker and single-pole or double-pole branch breakers.

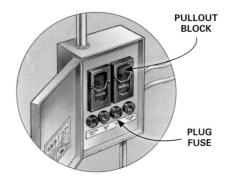

A fuse panel will usually have main pullout blocks with cartridge fuses and plug fuses for the branch circuits.

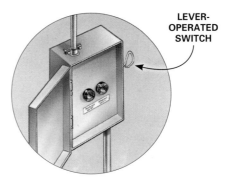

Auxiliary panels vary widely and may include lever-operated main switches with circuit breakers or cartridge or plug fuses.

replacing the fuse, identify and correct the problem.

A heavily used circuit that fails when you turn on a high-wattage appliance is probably overloaded. The solution is to move portable appliances to a different circuit with unused capacity.

If the circuit still fails, check for a short circuit or ground-fault condition. Unplug lamps and appliances and look for damaged plugs or cords.

Look for discoloration and smell for burned odors at receptacles, switches and fixtures. With lamps and appliances still unplugged, reset the breaker or replace the fuse. If the circuit fails again, there may be hidden problems in the house wiring. If the circuit fails only when you turn on a lamp or appliance, the problem may be corrected by repairing or replacing the item.

Circuit breakers

Single-pole breakers protect 120-volt lighting and appliance circuits usually rated at 15 or 20 amps.

Double-pole breakers protect 240-volt circuits rated at 15 to 50 amps, for appliances like clothes dryers and ranges.

Ground-fault circuit-interrupters (GFCI) protect people in damp locations from fatal electrical shocks.

Arc-fault circuit-interrupters (AFCI) de-energize bedroom and other circuits when arcing faults, such as damaged lamp cords, are detected.

Fuses

Standard Edison-base plug fuses (15 to 30 amp) can only be used as replacements in existing installations. Many local requirements mandate upgrading to type S plug fuses.

Time-delay plug fuses (15 to 30 amp) will tolerate the quick burst of a high motor-starting current without blowing and needing replacement.

Type S plug fuses and their matching permanent adapters prevent the wrong size fuses from being used.

Screw-in circuit breakers can replace existing standard plug fuses. When a breaker trips, its button can be reset. These can be replaced by type S fuses for safety.

Ferrule-type cartridge fuses, rated up to 60 amps, usually protect large-appliance circuits.

Knife-blade cartridge fuses, rated up to 600 amps, usually protect service or feeder wires.

Heating and cooling basics

Whole-house heating systems

Heating systems convert fuel or energy into heat and distribute it throughout the house. Regardless of the type, they all do the same job: keep our homes warm and comfortable. Heating systems differ mainly in the fuels they use and in the ways they generate and distribute the heat.

The most common whole-house systems are forced air and hot water. In both cases, air or a liquid is heated in a furnace or boiler and sent to the various parts of the house through ducts, pipes or tubes. The heated air in a forced-air system is blown into the rooms through ducts and registers. In hot-water systems, water or steam heats radiators, convectors or even the house's floors, ceilings or walls; these in turn give off their heat to the rooms. The furnace of a forced-air system and the boiler in the other systems have a burner that can be fueled by gas, oil, propane, butane, electricity, even wood or coal, depending upon their availability and the local preference.

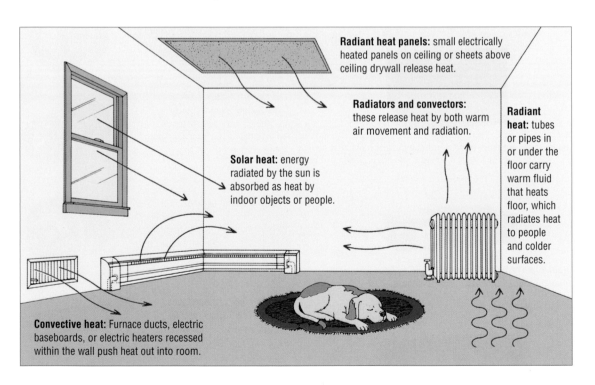

Radiant heat panels: small electrically heated panels on ceiling or sheets above ceiling drywall release heat.

Radiators and convectors: these release heat by both warm air movement and radiation.

Radiant heat: tubes or pipes in or under the floor carry warm fluid that heats floor, which radiates heat to people and colder surfaces.

Solar heat: energy radiated by the sun is absorbed as heat by indoor objects or people.

Convective heat: Furnace ducts, electric baseboards, or electric heaters recessed within the wall push heat out into room.

Common heating systems

System	Heat delivered by	Most common fuels	Means of distribution	Pros	Cons
Forced-air	Forced convection blower	Natural gas, fuel oil, propane, or electricity	Ductwork from furnace, electric heaters mounted on exterior walls or recessed into interior walls	Can also filter, humidify and air-condition. Rooms heat quickly. Wall heaters are inexpensive.	Large ductwork required. Fans can be noisy, can circulate mold and other allergens. Require regular filter changes.
Hot-water	Convection, or convection and radiation	Natural gas, fuel oil, propane, or electricity	Pipes and convectors or radiators	Efficient and quiet. Holds steady temperatures. Boiler can be small.	Slower temperature rise. Radiators or convectors take floor or wall space.
Steam	Convection, or convection and radiation	Natural gas, fuel oil, propane, or electricity	Pipes and radiators	Efficient and hot. Warms rooms quickly. Boilers can be small.	Can be noisy. Radiators can be hot to the touch. Boiler systems are tricky to maintain.
Radiant heat	Radiation, or radiation and convection	Gas, oil, propane, butane for floor systems; electricity for ceiling systems and exposed panels; wood and coal for stoves	Pipes or tubes in or under floors, wiring within plaster or above wallboard, panels mounted on ceilings or walls, firebox and flue pipe for stoves	Quiet, even heating. Embedded systems make floors pleasantly warm. Hydronic systems can use most-efficient energy source or fuel.	Slow to warm up and cool down. Expensive to install initially. Embedded elements or pipes are very difficult to repair.

Heat pumps extract heat from outside air and pump it indoors. Solar panels, fireplaces, wood-burning stoves and space heaters are also used. Generally, these heat sources provide auxiliary heat to supplement a whole-house system, although they may be all you need in warmer climates.

One or more thermostats control a whole-house system. The thermostat may also perform other functions, such as controlling the forced-air system blower fans or hot-water system valves.

Forced-air

Forced-air systems are relatively inexpensive to purchase and easy to maintain, making them one of the most popular types of whole-house heating. Because their design includes air ducts throughout the house, you have the option to add whole-house air-conditioning, humidification and air cleaning to the system.

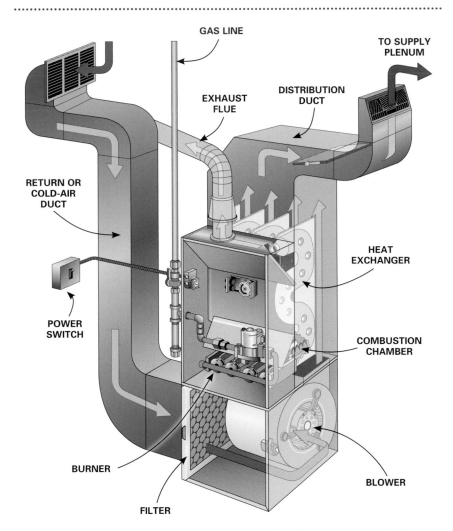

GAS LINE

TO SUPPLY
PLENUM

EXHAUST
FLUE

DISTRIBUTION
DUCT

RETURN OR
COLD-AIR
DUCT

HEAT
EXCHANGER

POWER
SWITCH

COMBUSTION
CHAMBER

BURNER

BLOWER

FILTER

How a furnace works. The thermostat sends a signal to the burner located inside the combustion chamber, which heats the outside of the heat exchanger. When the heat exchanger gets hot, the blower starts and pulls cool air into cold-air registers, through the cold-air return ducts, to the furnace. The return air goes through a filter to keep the blower clean. The air then passes through the inside of the heat exchanger, where it is warmed, safe from the burner combustion gases, which exit through the exhaust flue. Warm air is carried through the supply plenum and distribution ducts to warm-air supply registers in rooms.

A forced-air system contains five main elements: a furnace, a network of distribution ducts, registers on walls or floors, an exhaust flue and a thermostat. A motor-powered blower circulates air through the system. A few old furnaces still use gravity circulation, which relies on the natural convection created by the buoyancy of hot air and the fact that cold air falls. These systems have larger ducts and no blower.

Homes with ductwork can leak noticeably more air and require more heating and cooling energy than homes without ductwork. The reason is that forced air creates pressure differences within the house that can draw in outside air, force air out through cracks in the house or pull outside air in through cracks in the house, all of which waste heat.

To make sure your warm-air system works efficiently, clean or replace the filter regularly and follow the maintenance recommendations in the operating manual. Also, be sure your system has enough return ducts—at least one per level. In addition, seal all seams in ductwork, and insulate ducts in unheated spaces. For improved comfort, adjust dampers and registers to balance heat distribution. Some furnaces and thermostats allow you to run the blower constantly at a low speed. It costs more for the electricity to run the blower, but your house will be more comfortable and evenly heated, and your burner may run less.

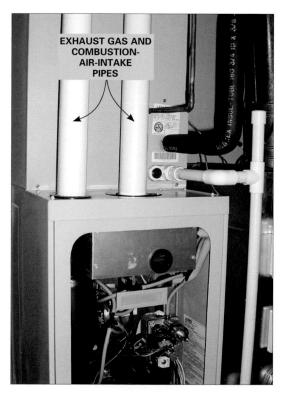

EXHAUST GAS AND COMBUSTION-AIR-INTAKE PIPES

High-efficiency furnaces

Top-of-the-line furnace models can operate at very high levels of efficiency—95 percent or more. Their design features a second heat exchanger to draw usable heat from the exhaust gases. The cooler exhaust gas can then be routed through a small vent, often of PVC pipe, through an outside wall—no conventional chimney is required. They also have a sealed combustion chamber and draw air from the outside, rather than inside. The downside is that the initial cost is greater and extra water-condensate from the exhaust must be piped or pumped to a drain.

Plumbing basics

We tend to take our plumbing for granted—until something clogs or starts leaking on a Saturday afternoon. That's when a little plumbing know—how pays off, both in dollars saved and convenience gained.

Your home's plumbing consists of two basic systems: a water-supply system and a drain/waste-vent (DWV) system. In the water-supply system, the water usually enters the house through a main service pipe and meter, unless you have a private well. Pressure, supplied by gravity from a local water tower or from a well pump, pushes the water through the system. Parallel supply lines carry hot and cold water to fixtures and appliances.

The DWV system is a separate set of nonpressurized pipes that carry water, waste and gases out of the house. Because the force of gravity carries off the waste, the horizontal drain pipes slope. Each main horizontal section of drain should contain cleanout plugs for removing blockages. At each fixture, the drainpipe contains a U-shaped trap, also called a P-trap, that traps water in its curve to create a seal that prevents sewer gas from escaping into the house. A toilet has a built-in P-trap.

The vent system, connected to the drainage system, allows sewer gases to escape, improves drainage, keeps P-trap seals in place and prevents water from backing up between fixtures.

Water-supply system

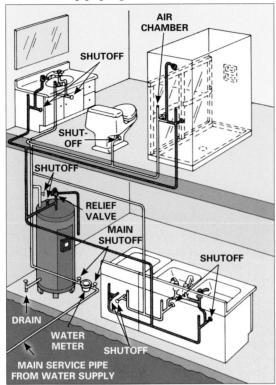

- AIR CHAMBER
- SHUTOFF
- SHUT-OFF
- SHUTOFF
- RELIEF VALVE
- MAIN SHUTOFF
- SHUTOFF
- DRAIN
- WATER METER
- SHUTOFF
- MAIN SERVICE PIPE FROM WATER SUPPLY

Drain/waste-vent system

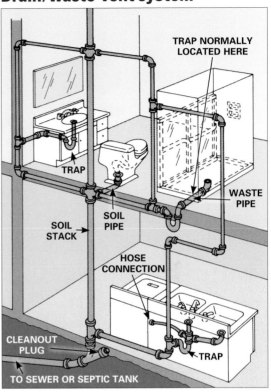

- TRAP NORMALLY LOCATED HERE
- TRAP
- WASTE PIPE
- SOIL STACK
- SOIL PIPE
- HOSE CONNECTION
- CLEANOUT PLUG
- TRAP
- TO SEWER OR SEPTIC TANK

Emergency shutoff valves

Shutoff valves allow you to control water flow to all or parts of the water-supply system to reduce damage from a supply leak or to make repairs or replace fixtures. The main shutoff, whether indoors or outdoors, is generally near where the service line enters the house, usually next to the meter. On a private system, it will be near where the line leaves the pressure tank. You'll also find shutoff valves at the water heater, boiler, individual fixtures and outdoor water lines.

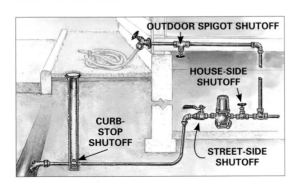

- OUTDOOR SPIGOT SHUTOFF
- HOUSE-SIDE SHUTOFF
- CURB-STOP SHUTOFF
- STREET-SIDE SHUTOFF

Main shutoff. This valve controls the flow of all water entering the water-supply system.

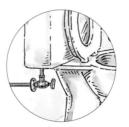

Toilet shutoff. This valve is usually on the cold water supply located underneath the tank.

Faucet shutoff. Separate valves control the hot and cold water.

Tile

Planning and prep tips

Laying tile is an excellent DIY home improvement project because you can start small and work your way up to larger, more complicated projects. One thing tile pros will tell you is that planning and preparation are key to a successful tile project.

Mock up and measure

Whether you're tiling a wall, floor or countertop, mock up and measure a row of tile to determine the layout. If you'll be using spacers to create grout lines, add them between the tiles before you measure. Use the measurement to determine whether you should shift the layout to get a wider tile in the corner, and to determine the layout for the end walls of a tub or shower.

SPACER

Start out level

Screw a straight board to a level line and stack tile on the board. When you've completed tiling above the board and the tiles are held firmly, remove the board and cut the first row of tile to fit. Leave a 1/8-in. space between the tub and the tile to allow installation of a flexible bead of caulk. This tip also allows you to wrap tile around tub corners as shown in the photo on p. 31.

Don't start the first row of tile by resting it against the tub or shower. It'll cause trouble because most tubs and showers aren't perfectly straight or level. Your tile will wander from the plumb line, and misaligned grout lines will be your only solution.

Do

PLUMB LINE

STRAIGHT, LEVEL BOARD

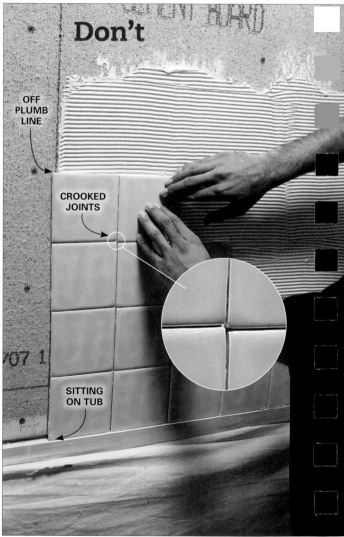

Don't

OFF PLUMB LINE

CROOKED JOINTS

SITTING ON TUB

Extend the row

Plan the tile layout so a column of tile extends past the end of the tub. Use the method shown in the bottom photo on p. 29 to determine how wide the corner tile needs to be in order to extend the tile beyond the tub. Plan to extend the tile 2 or 3 in. beyond the tub and to leave at least a half tile along the wall, if possible.

Don't stop tile even with the end of the tub. This leaves the walls along the front of the tub vulnerable to water damage, and doesn't look as finished as tile extending to the floor.

Do

NICE FIT

EXTEND
PAST
EDGE

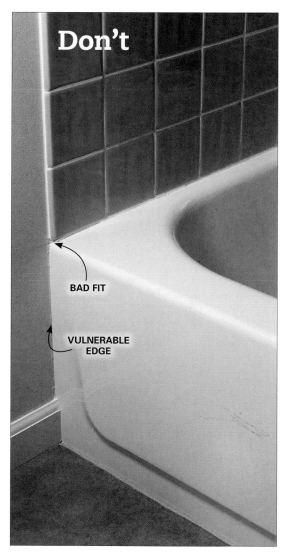

Don't

BAD FIT

VULNERABLE
EDGE

Plan layout to avoid skinny tiles

Locate the starting plumb line to leave the widest possible same-sized tiles at each corner. Lay out the tile on the floor and use the back wall measurement to determine how wide the corner tiles will be. If starting with the edge of a full tile in the center of the back wall leaves a skinny strip in the corner, shift the plumb line by half the width of the tile. This will increase the size of the corner tiles.

Don't leave a skinny strip of tile in the corners. Plan for the widest possible corner tile for the most attractive tile job.

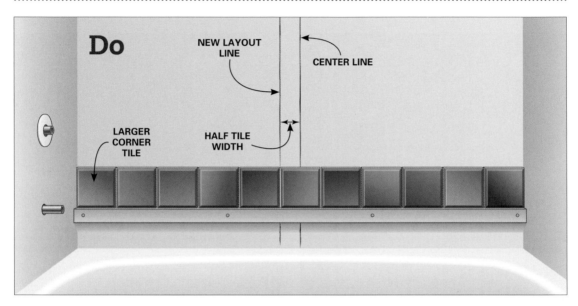

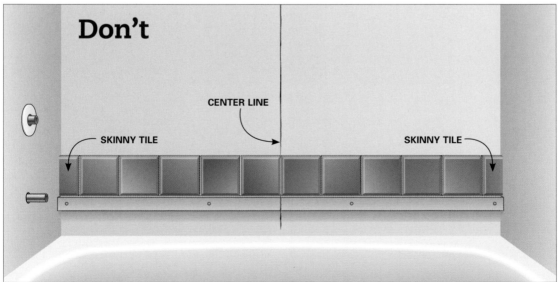

Waterproof wet areas

It's a surprise to most people that a tiled wall or floor isn't waterproof. Some types of tile are porous, and most grout isn't waterproof either. Water can seep through tile and grout and leak into cracks at corners and other intersections.

The only sure way to keep water from getting behind the tile is to waterproof all areas that may be exposed to water. Shown here is the RedGard brand, but there are others. A good rule of thumb is, "If in doubt, coat it with waterproofing."

Follow the application instructions on the container. Apply the waterproofer with an inexpensive paint pad because it works like a trowel, allowing you to quickly spread a thick, even layer over the surface.

PAINT PAD APPLICATOR

REDGARD

Cutting tips

Cutting tile can be intimidating, but you can do it with the right tools and guidance from our tile pros. If you've shied away from tile projects that required cutting, you may reconsider after reading these tips.

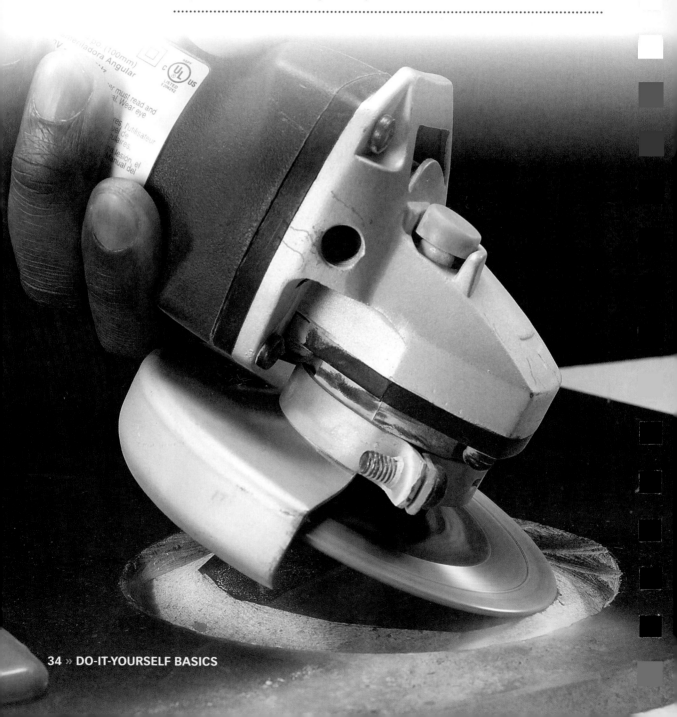

Cut tile with a grinder

Stone, porcelain and glass tiles offer beautiful options for bath and kitchen tiling projects. But cutting these hard materials presents a unique challenge. Straight cuts are easy to make with a diamond wet saw. But cutting curves and holes requires special techniques.

Here you'll learn how to use an inexpensive angle grinder with a diamond blade to cut perfect circles and squares in even the toughest tile. You can buy a 4-in. or 4-1/2-in. grinder and a dry-cut diamond blade to fit it for less than $100, In general, more expensive blades will last longer. When you're choosing a diamond blade, look for one with a continuous, rather than segmented rim for the smoothest cut.

Be aware, though, that cutting with a dry-cut diamond blade creates a lot of dust and noise. So make sure you cut in a well-ventilated area (or better yet, outside!) and wear hearing protection, a good-quality two-strap dust mask and safety glasses.

**SMOOTH
CONTINUOUS
RIM**

Tilt the blade for circles

Many tile jobs require you to cut one or more large round holes for floor drains or shower valves. Photos 1–3 show how to cut a hole for a shower valve. Shown here is how to cut a hole that's entirely within a single tile, one of the most difficult cuts. In the next section (p. 37) you'll see an easier method to use for cutting curves in the edge of a tile.

Even with this method, try to avoid a tile layout that places the edge of the circular cutout less than 1/2 in. from the edge of a tile. It's better to shift the entire layout instead. Otherwise, chances are good that you'll break the tile at the narrow point while cutting.

The method shown for cutting a circle with a grinder and diamond blade requires you to cut around the circle a number of times, making a deeper cut with each revolution. The key is to maintain the same angle and shave off progressive layers, moving the cut closer to the center of the circle (Photo 2).

....

SCORING CUT

RIGID FOAM BACKER

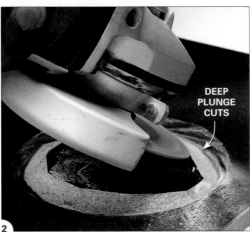

DEEP PLUNGE CUTS

1. Score the front of the tile along the circle guideline with the diamond blade. Tilt the grinder about 30 degrees and cut about 1/16 in. deep.

2. Move the blade 1/8 in. to the inside of the line and make a deeper cut. Continue moving the blade away from the line and cutting deeper until you cut completely through.

3. Grind off rough edges and trim back to the line for a perfect curve.

1. Score the profile with the saw, then cut in from the edge of the tile to remove as much waste as possible.

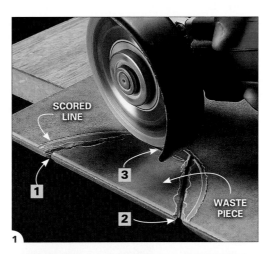

SCORED LINE

1

3

2

WASTE PIECE

1

2. Make a series of closely spaced cuts up to the scored line. Break off the waste. Then grind the edges smooth.

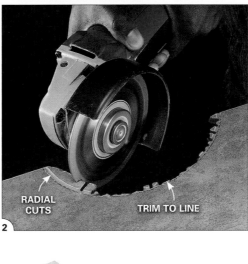

RADIAL CUTS

TRIM TO LINE

2

TILE NIPPER

Rough out semicircular cuts before trimming to the line

The process for cutting semicircles from the edge of tiles is similar to the technique shown on p. 36 for full circles. You start by marking the cut and scoring the face of the tile on the line. Then, rather than deepen the scoring cut, simply remove the excess tile with straight cuts (Photo 1).

Before you remove the excess tile (Photo 1), be sure to make short cuts on both sides of the semicircle (1 and 2). Then connect the cuts as shown (3). Rather than make this connecting cut in one pass, make a series of progressively deeper shallow cuts until you're through the tile.

Now complete the semicircle with a series of radial cuts—like the spokes of a wheel (Photo 2). Finish by cleaning up the rough edges with the diamond blade. Or remove the "tabs" with a tile nipper (a pliers-like biting tool). Then grind the edges smooth.

....

FRONT

BACK

TILE: CUTTING TIPS « 37

Make a dish-shaped cutout for small, rough holes

Most plumbing pipe holes are covered by a decorative escutcheon or hidden by a fixture base, so a precise round hole isn't necessary. Use the technique shown here to make rough, round holes.

Start by marking the circular cutout on the back of the tile. Then plunge the diamond blade down through the tile, keeping it centered on the hole so that the slot made by the blade extends equally on both sides of the circle marks (Photo 1). Check often to see when the slot through the front of the tile reaches the edges of the desired cutout. Then use the length of that plunge cut to gauge the diameter of a second, larger circle. Draw that larger circle on the back of the tile (Photo 2). Use this circle as a guide for making the rest of the plunge cuts. Rotate the grinder about a blade's width and make another plunge cut, stopping at the outer circle. Continue this process until you finish the hole.

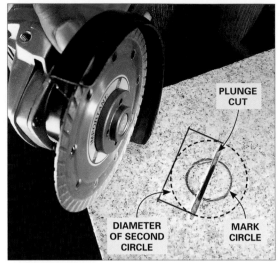

1. Center the cut on the hole and plunge slowly from the back. Stop when the slot through the face of the tile lines up with the edges of the desired cutout.

2. Draw another larger circle to guide the depth of the remaining cuts. Make repeated plunge cuts until the circle is complete.

Plunge-cut from the back to make square or rectangular cutouts

Cutting rectangular or square holes for electrical outlets is simple with this method. The key is to avoid cutting beyond the corners of the square where the cut might be visible. Plunge-cut slowly from the back and check often to avoid going too far.

....

1. Mark the cutout on the front and back of the tile precisely. Then score the front of the tile about 1/8 in. deep along the line.

2. Flip the tile over and plunge the cut from the back. Stop and check often. Stop when the cut lines up with the corners of the marked square on the front. Plunge-cut the remaining three sides.

Grouting tips

Grouting can be a rewarding task. It's the last step in a tile job, so you know you're almost done. And filling the joints with grout brings out the beauty of the tile. But if you've ever had grout turn rock hard before getting it off the tile, you know grouting can also be a nightmare. So to help you avoid problems and get the best results with the least effort, we've assembled these grouting tips.

Seal porous tile before grouting

If you don't seal porous tile and stone, grout will stick like glue and be nearly impossible to clean off. There are two different products that can make it easier to clean grout from porous stone and tile. If you're installing a matte finish tile or other tile with a rough or porous surface but don't want the sheen that a sealer would leave, apply a liquid grout release product. Grout release forms a thin film that prevents grout from sticking but washes off as you clean off the grout.

Use a sealer rather than grout release if you want to enhance the color of stone or leave a "wet" looking finish. You may have to apply another coat of sealer after grouting for maximum protection and to enhance the color of the stone.

Apply a thin coat of sealer to porous stone. Follow the application instructions on the label. Wipe up excess sealer with a cloth to avoid puddles. Then let the sealer dry before you grout.

Let the grout slake

It's tempting to skip this step, but it's important to let the grout set for 10 minutes after mixing. This step, called slaking, allows the water to completely moisten the dry ingredients. Remix the grout after the slaking period and adjust the mixture by adding a little more powder or water until you reach the viscosity of mayonnaise. Be careful, though—it doesn't take much of either to radically change the consistency.

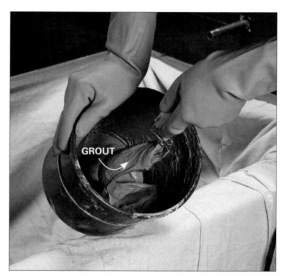

Remix the grout after letting it set for 10 or 15 minutes. Add a little water if the grout is too thick.

Force grout into the joints

For a long-lasting grout job, make sure all the joints are completely filled with grout. To accomplish this, make several passes over the same area from different directions with the grout float. Hold the float with its face at an angle of about 45 degrees to the tile to force the grout into the joint. When the joints are filled, remove excess grout from the face of the tiles by holding the float at almost 90 degrees to the tile and scraping it off.

Fill the joints by pushing the grout at an angle to the joints with a grout float. Start in one corner and work methodically to fill all the joints.

Don't spread too much grout at once

Temperature and humidity affect how quickly grout starts to harden after you spread it on the wall. And once it does start to harden, you'll really have to hustle to get it cleaned off the tile and get the joints shaped before the grout turns rock hard. Avoid this problem by grouting small areas at a time. Start by spreading grout onto a 3 x 3-ft. area. Finish grouting, shaping the joints and cleaning each section before proceeding.

Scoop grout from the bucket with your grout float and apply it to the wall with upward strokes. Don't worry about getting it into the joints yet.

Tool the joints

Shape and compact the grout by dragging a tool across every joint. The tool can be anything from the rounded corner of the grout float to the rounded end of a toothbrush handle. Whatever is handy and has about the right radius to create a slightly concave joint will work. Don't use metal tools. They can damage the tile or leave marks.

Pull the rounded corner of the grout float over every joint to shape them.

Use a clean, damp sponge to remove grout

Start with a clean bucket of water. Wet your grouting sponge and wring it out until it's just damp. Then, starting along one side of the grouted area, position the sponge so that the corner of one long side of the sponge is in contact with the wall and drag the sponge in a continuous stroke up the wall. Now rotate the sponge to expose a clean corner and repeat the process alongside the first stroke. When you've used all four corners of the sponge, rinse it in clean water, wring it out, and continue the process until you've cleaned the entire area once. Clean the tiles two or three more times using the same process until they're free of grout residue. A thin film of grout may appear when the water evaporates. Buff this off with a soft cloth.

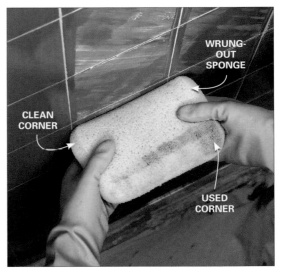

Remove grout from the face of the tile with the corner of a damp sponge. Swipe from bottom to top, using a clean corner of the sponge for each stroke.

Don't scrub the grout or use too much water

Let the grout harden slightly before you clean off the excess. Test the grout by pressing on it with your finger. When it's hard enough to resist denting, you can start cleaning the excess grout from the face of the tile and shaping the joints. Two common mistakes at this point are using too much water, and scrubbing the tile like you're washing a wall. Too much water will weaken the tile and cause the grout color to be uneven when it dries. And scrubbing doesn't remove grout efficiently; it just moves it around.

Remove grout from corners before caulking

Because it's flexible and can handle slight movement, caulk is used at corners instead of grout. For a good tile installation, apply a neat bead of matching caulk at vulnerable areas like along the tub or countertop and at inside corners. But to achieve a good-quality caulk joint, you'll first have to remove the grout from these areas. Most home centers and tile shops will have caulk to match the color of your grout.

Don't

DRIPPING WATER

Don't use a dripping wet sponge to clean grout from the tile. If water runs down, the sponge is too wet.

REMOVE GROUT

Remove grout from inside corners and along the tub to make room for caulk. Use a utility knife for narrow spaces or an old screwdriver or putty knife for wider joints.

Tile goofs

Cat'll call

After living in our old house for years, we decided to go all out and remodel the bathroom. Our dream was to install a Jacuzzi tub with a beautiful tile surround. After all the backbreaking work, we finally got to the fun part—setting the tile. We did a flawless job! Later that evening, we realized our cat was missing. After looking everywhere, we

heard a distinct meow coming from the bathroom. Realizing that the sound was corning from the new tub surround, we carefully cut through the tile and cement board and found our cat alive and well. We made the best of a bad situation—our rescue hole became a maintenance access panel that we probably should have installed in the first place.

Unplanned shower

Last year my fiancee and I started our first home improvement project together, aptly, a shower. We installed a new control valve along with new tile. Although my fiancee was still grouting the tile, I decided it was safe to turn on the main water supply valve because we'd finished the plumbing. A second later, a scream echoed through the house. I ran to the bathroom and saw that the shower was blasting on my fiancee. We'd left the valve in the open position and she couldn't turn it off because we hadn't installed the handles. Anyway, a year after this first shower, we're happily married!

Modern tricks for modern tile

Tile just keeps getting bigger and bigger—in popularity and in size. The materials have changed too: Ceramic is still around, but porcelain and glass are now almost as common. Our tile guru, Dean Sorem, has had to change how he works. Here are some of his tips.

1. **Pick a large-notched trowel for big tile.** Tiles as large as 2 ft. square have become more popular, and these monsters require a deep layer of thin-set to allow for adjustments. To get the right amount of thin-set, use a 1/2 x 1/2-in. notched trowel for tiles up to 16 in. square, and a 3/4 x 3/4-in. notched trowel for larger tiles. Don't forget: Using large-notched trowels means you'll need a lot more thin-set. As a general rule, a 50-lb. bag of thin-set will cover about 40 to 50 sq. ft. using a 1/2 x 1/2-in. notched trowel, and about 30 to 40 sq. ft. using a 3/4 x 3/4-in. notched trowel. When you use large-notched trowels like this, look for thin-set labeled "medium bed," "large tile" or "large format."

1/2" x 1/2" NOTCHED TROWEL

MEDIUM-BED THIN-SET

3/4" x 3/4" NOTCHED TROWEL

2. **Flatten the framing.** Old-school tile setters made up for wavy walls by installing wire lath and floating a layer of mortar over it. But modern tile backer boards simply follow along the crooked wall, and if you don't fix the wall, you'll have a wavy tile job.

The best solution is to straighten the walls before you install the backer board. Lay a straightedge against the walls to find high and low spots. In most cases, you can fix problems by adding shims to the face of the studs until the faces all line up. But if you have just one protruding stud, then it may be quicker to plane it down with a power planer or replace it if you can.

Dean prefers thin paper shims as shown (available in the drywall section of some home centers) because they provide precise control over shim thickness and can be offset to create a tapered shim. You can make your own thin shims from heavy felt paper or thin cardboard. Staple the shims in place.

CARDBOARD SHIMS

3. Cut without cracking the tile. You'll need a diamond wet saw to cut large porcelain tiles. Dean recommends renting a contractor-quality saw rather than buying a cheapie. But even with a saw like this, tiles larger than about 8 in. square have a tendency to crack before you finish the cut, often ruining the tile. You can help prevent this by pressing the two pieces together as you near completion of the cut. Holding the tile like this stabilizes it and dampens vibration, resulting in a cleaner cut.

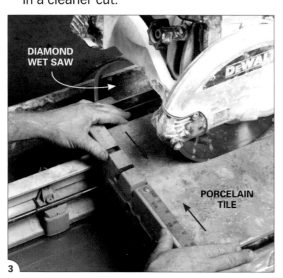

DIAMOND WET SAW

PORCELAIN TILE

3

4. Back-butter large tile. The increased surface area of tiles larger than about 8 x 8 in. makes it critical that you butter the back to ensure a strong bond. It takes only a few extra seconds per tile to spread a thin layer of thin-set on the back of the tile with the flat side of the trowel. Then when you set the tile, this thin layer bonds easily with the layer you've troweled onto the floor or wall and creates a strong connection.

Dean also butters the back of larger transparent glass tiles to provide a consistent color. Otherwise you'll see air bubbles and other imperfections in the thin-set through the transparent glass.

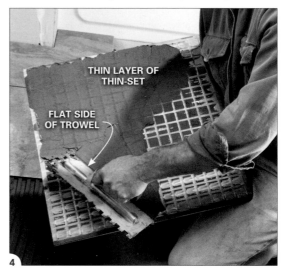

THIN LAYER OF THIN-SET

FLAT SIDE OF TROWEL

4

5. Flatten thin-set before installing mosaic tile. Mosaic tile is typically thin, and it has a lot of grout joints. If you simply apply thin-set with a notched trowel and embed the sheets of mosaic in it, the ridges of thin-set will squeeze out of all those grout joints and you'll have a real mess to clean up.

The way to avoid this is to flatten the ridges with the flat side of the trowel before you set the mosaic tiles in it. Use the notched side of a 1/4 x 1/4-in. V-notched trowel first to apply the right amount of thin-set. Then flip the trowel over to the flat side and, holding the trowel fairly flat to the surface and using medium pressure, flatten the ridges. Now you can safely embed the sheets of mosaic tile without worrying about thin-set filling the grout joints.

6. Upgrade your grout sponge. It's hard to get the last bit of grout haze off using a grout sponge. After the grout dries, you usually have to come back and polish off the remaining cloudy layer with a rag. But if you finish your grout cleanup with a microfiber sponge, you'll end up with a job so clean you may not have to do anything more.

Start your cleanup with the plain side of the sponge after the grout firms up. Then when the joints are nicely shaped and most of the grout is off the face of the tile, switch to the microfiber side of the sponge. You'll find microfiber sponges at home centers and tile shops.

GROUT HAZE

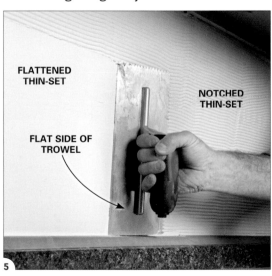

FLATTENED THIN-SET

NOTCHED THIN-SET

FLAT SIDE OF TROWEL

5

6

MICROFIBER SPONGE

7. **Clean grout joints with a toothbrush.** No matter how careful you are, you're bound to end up with some thin-set in the joints between tiles. And if you allow it to harden, it'll interfere with your grout job. A toothbrush works great to clean excess thin-set from grout joints, especially for the skinny joints between mosaic tiles. Let the thin-set get firm, but not hard, before you start the cleanup process. If you try to clean up thin-set too soon, you risk disturbing the tiles.

8. **Make a custom trowel.** Dean has discovered that inexpensive auto-body filler spatulas, available at home centers and auto parts stores, are perfect for making custom trowels for special circumstances. One way Dean uses a custom-made trowel is for insetting thinner tiles into a field of thicker tiles. After finishing the field tile installation, he cuts notches on each edge of the spatula with a utility knife to create a mini screed. He cuts the notches about 1/16 in. deeper than the thickness of the decorative tile to allow for thin-set. Then he uses this trowel to add a layer of thin-set that acts as a shim when it hardens (top photo). After this layer hardens, he cuts 3/16-in.-deep teeth in the spatula to make a notched trowel and uses it to apply thin-set (middle photo). Now when he sets the decorative tile, it's perfectly flush with the field tile (bottom photo).

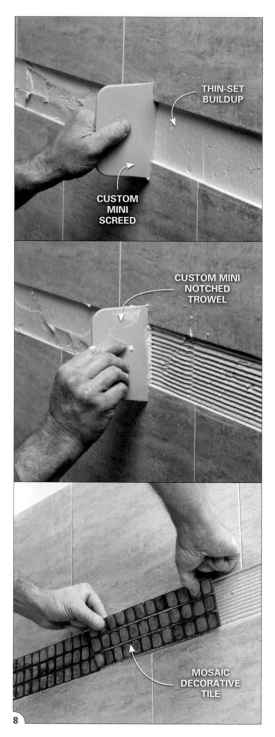

THIN-SET BUILDUP

CUSTOM MINI SCREED

CUSTOM MINI NOTCHED TROWEL

MOSAIC DECORATIVE TILE

9. Finish your job with premium grout.
There's been a revolution in grout technology, and all of the big-name grout producers have modern grout that's easier to apply, denser, more stain resistant and more colorfast than standard grout. These grouts also cure faster and are resistant to mold and mildew.

You no longer have to mix in latex additives, worry about uneven or blotchy grout joints or decide between sanded and unsanded grout. Power Grout, Custom Building Product's Prism and Fusion Pro grouts, and Laticrete's PermaColor are a few examples of premium grout. You may have to visit a specialty tile store to find them, though. The formulas vary, but all of these will outperform standard grout. And some, like Power Grout and Fusion Pro, don't even require sealing, saving you time and money.

Premium grouts are more expensive, of course, and might add a little to the total cost of your project. But considering all the other costs (and all your hard work), premium grout is a bargain.

9

10. Level mosaic tile with a block. Mosaic tiles are so small and numerous that getting their faces flush using just your fingers is nearly impossible. But tamping them with a flat block of wood creates a perfectly aligned surface in no time. Make a tamping block out of any flat scrap of wood. An 8-in. length of hardwood 1x6 or a 6 x 8-in. rectangle of plywood is perfect. After you set several square feet of mosaic tile, pat the tile into the thin-set with the tamping block. Hold the block in place and bump it with your fist to flatten the mosaic. Repeat the tamping process on each new section of tile you install.

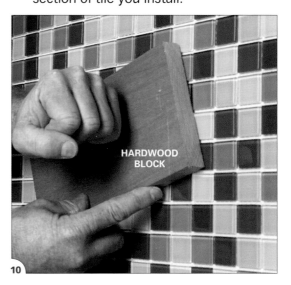

HARDWOOD BLOCK

10

PROFESSIONAL
COST: $450

YOUR COST: $150

SAVINGS: $300

COMPLEXITY
Moderate

TOOLS
Screwdriver

Bucket

Caulk gun

Drill/driver

Grout float

Level

Non-contact voltage
  tester

Notched towel

Rubber mallet

Tape measure

Utility knife

MATERIALS
Caulk

Grout

Grout sealer

Mastic

Outlet extenders

Tile

Tile spacers

How to tile a backsplash

Nothing packs more style per square inch than mosaic tile. So if your kitchen's got the blahs, give it a quick infusion of pizzazz with a tile backsplash. Because the small tiles are mounted on 12 x 12-in. sheets, installation is fast. You can install the tile on Saturday and then grout it on Sunday.

Shown here are slate tiles, which sometimes crumble when you cut them. Other types of mosaic tile, especially ceramic tiles, are easier to cut.

Here you'll learn how to install the tile sheets. You'll need basic tile tools, available at home centers and tile stores, including a 3/16-in. trowel and a grout float. You'll also need mastic adhesive, premium grout and grout sealer. You can rent a wet saw to cut the tiles.

Prepare the walls

Before installing the tile, clean up any grease splatters on the wall (mastic won't adhere to grease). Wipe the stains with a sponge dipped in a mixture of water and mild dishwashing liquid (Dawn works well). If you have a lot of stains or they won't come off, wipe on a paint deglosser with a lint-free cloth or abrasive pad so the mastic will adhere. Deglosser is available at paint stores and home centers.

Then mask off the countertops and any upper cabinets that will have tile installed along the side. Leave a 1/4-in. gap between the wall and the tape for the tile (Photo 1). Cover the countertops with newspaper or a drop cloth.

Turn off power to the outlets in the wall and remove the cover plates. Make sure the power is off with a noncontact voltage detector. Place outlet extenders in the outlet boxes. The National Electrical Code requires extenders when the boxes are more than 1/4 in. behind

1. Mark a centerline between the upper cabinets so the tiles will be centered under the vent hood. Screw a ledger board to the wall to support the tile.

the wall surface. It's easier to put in extenders now and cut tile to fit around them than to add them later if the tile opening isn't big enough. Set the extenders in place as a guide for placing the tile. You'll remove them later for grouting.

On the wall that backs your range, measure down from the top of the countertop backsplash a distance that's equal to three or four full rows of tile (to avoid cutting the tile) and make a mark. Screw a scrap piece of wood (the ledger board) to the wall at the mark between the cabinets.

The area between the range and the vent hood is usually the largest space on the wall—and certainly the most seen by the cooks in the house—so it'll serve as your starting point for installing the tile. Make a centerline on the wall halfway between the cabinets and under the vent hood (Photo 1). Measure from the centerline to the cabinets. If you'll have to cut tile to fit, move the centerline slightly so you'll only have to cut the mesh backing (at least on one side).

2. Spread a thin layer of mastic adhesive on the wall, starting at the centerline. Spread just enough adhesive for two or three sheets at a time so the adhesive doesn't dry before you set the tile.

Install and seal the tile

Using a 3/16-in. trowel, scoop some mastic adhesive out of the tub and put it on the wall (no technique involved here!). Spread the mastic along the centerline, cutting in along the ledger board, vent hood and upper cabinets (Photo 2). Then use broad strokes to fill in the middle. Hold the trowel at a 45-degree angle to the wall to spread the mastic thin—you should be able to see the layout lines where the points of the trowel touch the wall. Have a water bucket and sponge on hand to keep the trowel clean. Whenever the mastic starts to harden on the trowel, wipe it off with the wet sponge.

Place plastic tile spacers on the ledger board and countertop. This leaves a gap so the tiles don't sit directly on the countertop (you'll caulk the gap later).

Align the first tile sheet with the centerline, directly over the spacers. Press it onto the wall with your hand. If the sheet slides around and mastic comes through the joint lines, you're applying the mastic too thick (remove the sheet, scrape off some mastic and retrowel). Scrape out any mastic in the joints with a utility knife.

Eyeball a 1/16-in. joint between sheets of tile (you don't need spacers). After every two or three installed sheets, tap them into the mastic with a board and rubber mallet (Photo 3).

3. Tap the tile into the mastic with a wood scrap and a rubber mallet. Stand back, look at the tiles and straighten any crooked ones.

If tiles fall off the sheets, dab a little mastic on the back and stick them right back in place. The sheets aren't perfectly square, so you may need to move individual tiles to keep joints lined up. Move the tiles with your fingers or by sticking a utility knife blade in the joint and turning the blade. If an entire sheet is crooked, place a grout float over the tile and move the sheet. You'll have about 20 minutes after installing the tile to fine-tune it.

If you're lucky, you can fit the tile sheets under upper cabinets and around outlets by cutting the mesh backing with a utility knife. If not, you'll have to cut the tile with a wet saw. Nippers and grinders cause the slate tiles to shatter or crumble, although you can use these tools on ceramic tile.

Slice the backing to the nearest full row of tile, install the sheet around the outlet or next to the cabinet, then cut tiles with a wet saw to fill the gaps (Photo 4). Cut the tiles while they're attached to the sheet. Individual tiles are too small to cut (the blade can send them flying!).

Let the tile sit for at least 30 minutes, then apply a grout sealer if you're using natural stone (like slate) or unglazed quarry tile. The sealer keeps the grout from sticking to the tile (it's not needed for nonporous tiles such as ceramic). Pour the sealer on a sponge, then wipe on just enough to dampen the tiles.

Grout and clean the tile

Wait 24 hours after installing the tile to add the grout. Use a premium grout that has a consistent color and resists stain. Since the backsplash will be subject to splatters and stains from cooking and food prep, spend the extra money for a premium grout. You can find or special-order it at home centers or tile stores. Sanded grout will also work and will save you a few bucks.

Mix the grout with water until it reaches mashed potato consistency, then put some on the wall with a grout float. Work the grout into the joints by moving the float diagonally over the tiles (Photo 5). Hold the grout float at a 45-degree angle to the tile. Scrape off excess grout with the float after the joints are filled.

Ten minutes after grouting, wipe the grout off the surface of the tiles with a damp sponge. If the

4. Cut tile sheets to the nearest full row to fit around outlets, then fill the gaps with tiles cut on a wet saw.

5. Force grout into the joints with a float. Scrape off excess grout by moving the float diagonally across the tile.

grout pulls out of the joints, wait another 10 minutes for it to harden. Continually rinse the sponge in a bucket of water and wipe the tiles until they're clean.

These slate tiles have a lot of crevices that retain grout. While most of the grout comes off the tiles with the wet sponge, some won't. Most pro installers leave some grout in slate and other rough-surface tile—it's just part of the deal with some types of natural stone. But if you want the tile completely clean, remove the grout from individual tiles with a toothbrush.

After cleaning the wall, use a utility knife to rake the grout out of the joints along the bottom of the backsplash and in the inside corners (Photo 6). These expansion joints allow the wall to move without cracking the grout.

Two hours after grouting, wipe the haze off the tiles with microfiber cloths. Then caulk the expansion joints with latex caulk. Use a colored caulk that closely matches the grout.

After seven days, sponge on a grout sealer to protect the grout against stains.

That's it! Now every time your family and friends gather in your kitchen, they'll be impressed with your custom backsplash.

6

6. Rake the grout out of the joints at inside corners and along the bottom with a utility knife so you can fill them with caulk. Keep the dull side of the blade along the countertop.

Carpet

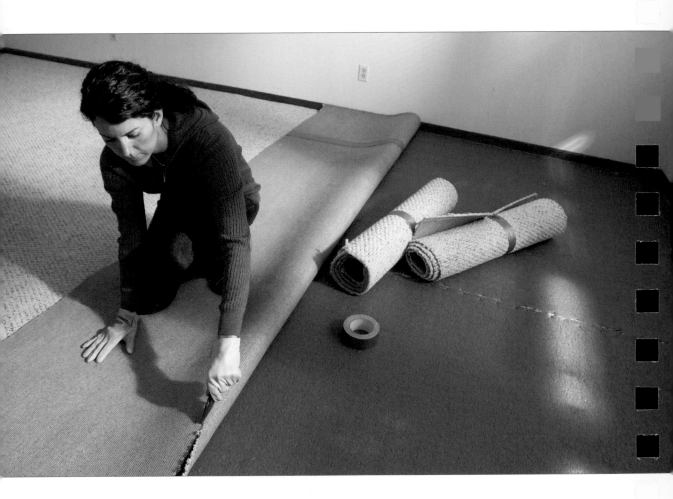

How to carpet a basement floor

PROFESSIONAL COST:
$3,000 for 200 sq. ft.

YOUR COST: $2,000
for 200 sq. ft.

SAVINGS: $1,000
for 200 sq. ft.

COMPLEXITY
Moderate

TOOLS
Circular saw
Cordless drill
Hammer

MATERIALS
6-mil poly sheeting
Concrete screws
Plywood
Vapor barrier tape

For basement floors, assume that the concrete floor will get damp at some point. You then have two options, depending on your circumstances. Both of the options use the same layers of 1/2-in. plywood, carpet pad and carpet as shown here. It's the initial layer that differs.

The solution on the right (Option B) will work on a concrete floor that has no persistent dampness, seepage or leakage. The 6-mil layer of plastic helps to minimize potential moisture migration up into the plywood.

Option A can be applied on concrete where there's a higher risk of some dampness. The initial layer is a durable high-density polyethylene sheet (called Delta-FL) that uses evenly spaced 3/8-in. tall dimples to create air space and a moisture barrier between the concrete and the plywood.

Lay the sheet over the concrete floor (dimples down), overlap adjacent edges and tape the seams. Add the plywood layer on top and anchor it to the concrete with 15 concrete screws (predrilled and countersunk) per 4 x 8-ft. sheet.

You can buy Delta-FL in 4 x 8-ft. sheets or in a 5 x 65-1/2 ft. roll. Visit dorken.com for more information on this product.

Before you proceed, consult a local building inspector to determine specific building codes for this type of project. Also, be sure your basement floor is level. Finally, note that these options will raise your floor by 1-1/4 to 1-1/2 in., so make sure this added height won't create problems with doors and floor transitions.

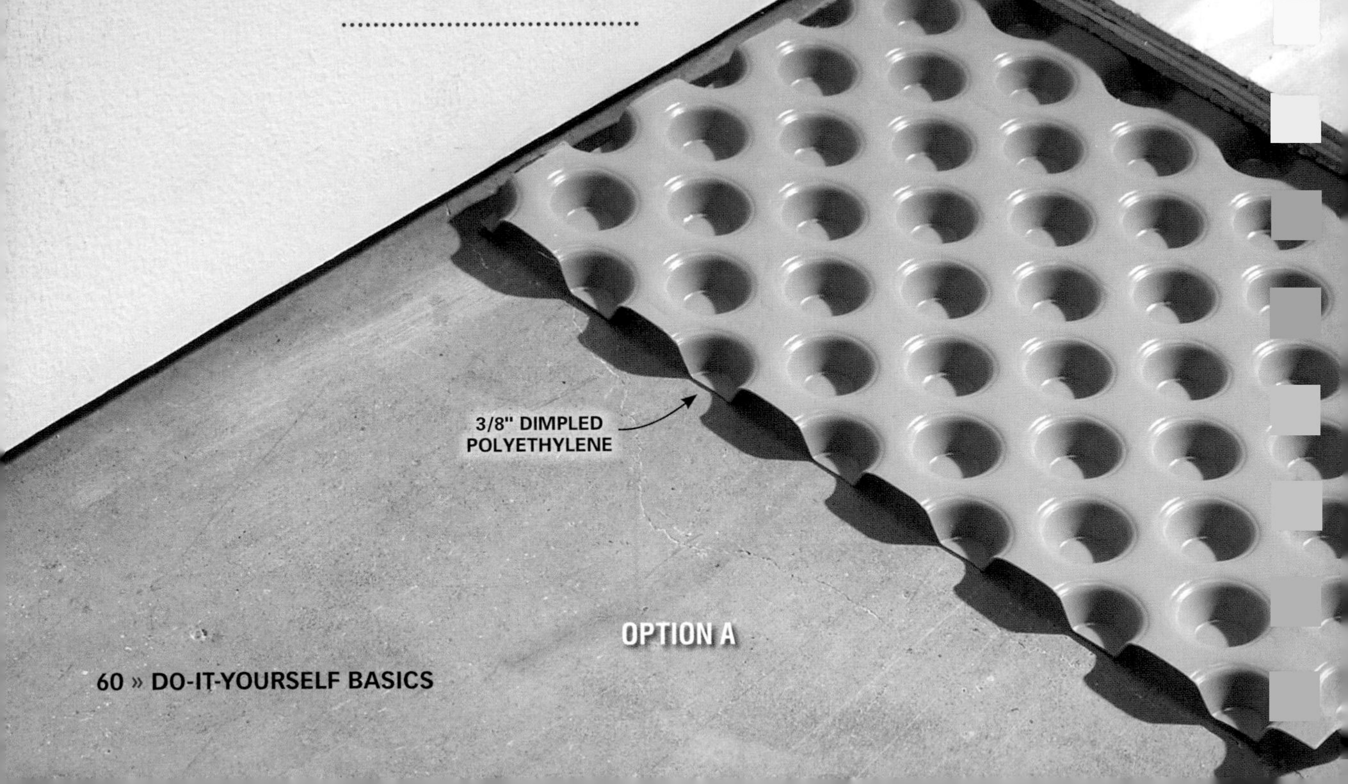

3/8" DIMPLED POLYETHYLENE

OPTION A

PAD

TACK
STRIP

1/2"
PLYWOOD

CONCRETE
SCREW

6-MIL
PLASTIC

OPTION B

Restretch a carpet

PROFESSIONAL COST: $200

YOUR COST: $50

SAVINGS: $150

COMPLEXITY
Simple

TOOLS
Carpet cutter
Cold chisel
Flat-head screwdriver
Hammer
Knee kicker
Needle-nose pliers
Power carpet strecher
Pry bar
Rubber mallet
Stapler
Tin snips
Utility knife

MATERIALS
5/16" in. staples

Tack strips

Don't be afraid to pull up carpeting during a remodel or cabinet construction. Fitting, trimming and restretching it isn't difficult. With a few special rented tools and the coaching in this article, you can do a great job even if it's your first try. The techniques we show also work to get rid of wrinkles. But don't go into it thinking you'll save a boatload of money. The big advantage is that you can get the room back in order on your schedule rather than idling on a carpet layer's backlogged customer list (or taking off work to keep the appointment).

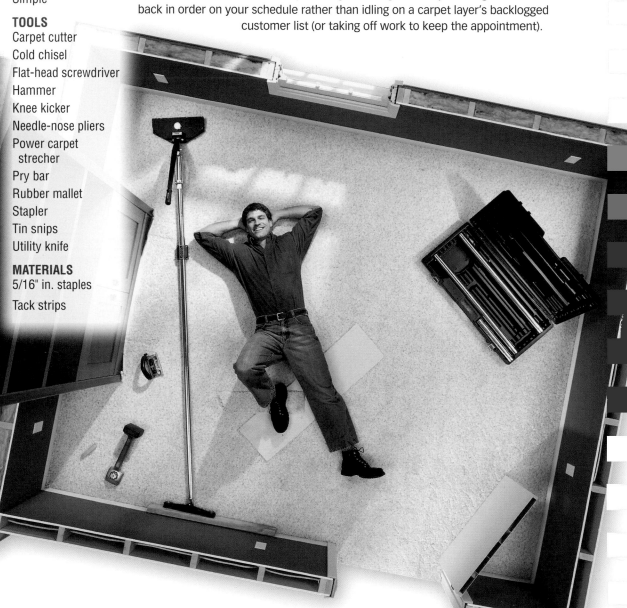

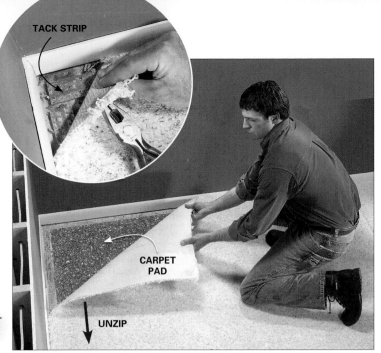

TACK STRIP

CARPET PAD

UNZIP

1. Lift a corner of the carpeting free of the tack strip with pliers and then peel back the carpet. Once it's started, it'll release easily, like pulling on a zipper.

PADDING STAPLES

2. Dig the staples out of the carpet pad with a screwdriver or needle-nose pliers. Be patient and get them all. Otherwise the pad will rip.

quick tip!

➤ If you only need to remove wrinkles, skip all of the business on taking up and re-laying the carpet and just use the techniques we show in Photo 8 and the stretching sequences we show on p. 67.

You may be tempted to build your new bookcase or other project on top of the carpet. Resist the urge! It'll just make your construction work and future carpet replacement harder, not to mention the risk of damaging the carpet while you're working.

While the techniques we show are similar to the ones used for installing new carpeting, we don't recommend installing large tracts of new carpeting yourself. Seaming, layout and carpet hauling are best left to the pros. And compared with the price of new pad and carpet, pro installation fees are relatively cheap.

Rent three key tools

The most important tool to rent is a "power" stretcher (Photo 8). It does the lion's share of the stretching. If you have tight areas where the power stretcher won't fit (spaces less than 3 ft. from adjoining walls), you'll also need to rent a "knee kicker." If a carpet cutter is available, rent it, too (Photo 10). It'll cut off carpet edges more cleanly and accurately than a utility knife. In addition to these tools, you'll need a pry bar to remove the tack strip (Photo 3), a stapler with 5/16-in. staples to reinstall the pad, and tin snips or a chisel to cut the new tack strips to length (Photo 4).

Pull back the carpet and pad

Lift one corner of the carpet with a pair of pliers and gently tease it free of the tack strip (Photo 1). But be careful; it's easy to unravel the fibers. Then you'll be able to grab hold of the carpet and pull it away from all the tack strips like a zipper. Also be careful not to pull the carpet past doorways where you might break a seam. If this happens, you'll have to hire a pro to come and fix it.

Before you pull back the pad, pull out all of the staples with a screwdriver and pliers (Photo 2). Don't pull the pad through the staples, or it will rip.

If you have any pesky floor squeaks, this is the perfect

pro tips!

➤ Before you run to the rental store to pick up your carpet stretching tools, have the tack strips installed and the pad stapled down. Chances are you'll only need the tools for a few hours, so you want to be ready to use them right away to save on rental fees.

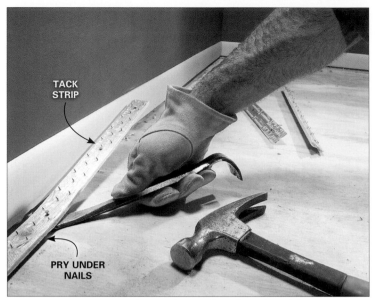

TACK STRIP

PRY UNDER NAILS

3. Pry out as many 4-ft. sections of tack strip with a pry bar as needed to clear a built-in cabinet. Then discard them.

NEW BUILT-IN CABINET

TIN SNIPS

4. Cut new tack strips to length with a pair of tin snips. Wear gloves to protect your hands from the needle-sharp tacks.

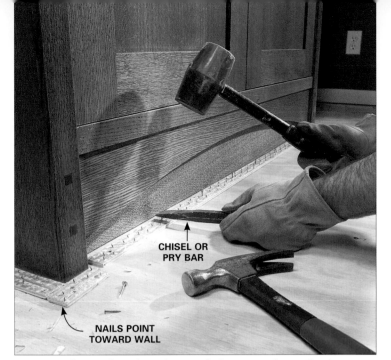

CHISEL OR PRY BAR

NAILS POINT TOWARD WALL

5. Space the tack strips about 1/2 in. away from the baseboards and nail them into place with the gripping nails pointing toward the walls. Use a cold chisel or pry bar and mallet to sink nails under toe-kicks.

CUT AT CORNERS FIRST

6. Use a utility knife to cut the padding to fit tightly against the tack strip. Then staple the padding back in place with 5/16-in. staples spaced about every 3 in. around the perimeter and along the seams.

time to take care of them. Walk around the room with a keen ear and mark the squeaks on the floor. Fix them by screwing the subfloor to underlying floor joists with 2-1/2 in. screws. Now is the time to install any new built-ins.

Remove and replace tack strips

Tack strips have prestarted setting nails that secure them to the floor and needle-sharp nails driven at slight angles that grip the carpet after it's stretched (Photo 3). Wear gloves when handling tack strips or you'll have blood on your hands! If you have a wooden floor, pull up and discard as many 4-ft. tack strip sections as needed to clear the base of your project. It's easiest to pry them up by pounding a pry bar under the setting nails (Photo 3).

If you have tack strips in a concrete floor, carefully lay out your project's footprint on the floor and chisel through the tack strips just outside the layout marks. Then pry out the wood through the concrete nails (they won't pull out) and break off the nails by hitting them sideways with a hammer. Breaking off the concrete nails will probably leave craters in the concrete, which makes it hard to drive in new ones.

Make sure to point the carpet-gripping nail tips toward the wall when you install them (Photo 5) or they won't hold the carpet in place during stretching. Position them half the thickness of the carpet away from the wall (e.g., 3/4-in. thick carpet, 3/8 in. away from wall). Installing them is simply a matter of driving the prestarted setting nails into the floor with a hammer. Don't leave any gaps at corners or between lengths.

Tack strips always come in 4-ft. lengths and are available with concrete nails for slabs or standard nails for wooden floors, so be sure to get the right kind. Cut the strips to length with tin snips (Photo 4). If you can't get at the setting nails because of an overlying toe-kick or an overhang, pull them out and set the tack strip in a bed of construction adhesive. But wait overnight for the glue to set before stretching the carpet. Or use a cold chisel or flat bar as we show in Photo 5.

Rough-cut around obstacles

When you're ready to reinstall the carpet, trim the pad so it rests right next to the tack strips and staple it every 3 in. or so along the seams and the tack strip (Photo 6). Then roll the carpet against any built-ins and make diagonal cuts away from the corner (Photo 7). Then cut off all but 3 in. of the excess with a utility knife. Work from the underside to make cutting easier. You'll cut off the 3-in. overlap after stretching, as we show in Photo 10.

ANGLE-CUT AWAY FROM CORNER

7. Mark the carpet at outside corners and cut angled clearance cuts with a utility knife. Then trim off most of the excess carpet, leaving about 3 in. extra along each side.

EMBED IN TACK STRIP

POWER STRETCHER

8. Plant the power stretcher against the opposite baseboard and add extension sections until the gripping head is about 6 in. away from the wall. Push down on the lever and embed the carpet backing on the tack strips with your hand. Follow the sequence on the next page.

Stretching sequence

Step 1 Power-stretch the length

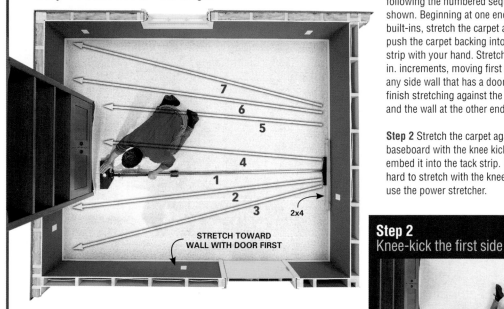

STRETCH TOWARD
WALL WITH DOOR FIRST

2x4

Step 1 Power-stretch the length first, following the numbered sequence shown. Beginning at one end of any built-ins, stretch the carpet and then push the carpet backing into the tack strip with your hand. Stretch in 18-in. increments, moving first toward any side wall that has a door. Then finish stretching against the built-in and the wall at the other end.

Step 2 Stretch the carpet against the baseboard with the knee kicker and embed it into the tack strip. If it's too hard to stretch with the knee kicker, use the power stretcher.

Step 2
Knee-kick the first side

Step 3 Power-stretch the last side

Step 4
Knee-kick the tight areas

Step 3 Stretch the opposite side of the room with the power stretcher. Start stretching beginning a foot or so behind the point where the carpet was rolled back.

Step 4 Knee-kick the tight areas, working from the front of the built-in toward the wall.

Using a power stretcher

The power stretcher kit (Photo 8) comes with extension sections so you can adjust the shaft length to the room dimensions. It works by bracing one end against a wall while you embed the teeth of the head in the carpet about 6 in. away from the unanchored edge. As you force the lever down, the teeth dig through the surface fibers, grip the carpet backing and stretch the carpet. Before you release the handle, push the carpet into the tack strip directly in front of the head. Protect the wall or woodwork by resting the "pushing" end against a short length of 2x4 (see the stretching sequence on p. 67).

The dial on the power head determines how deep the teeth dig into the carpet. The deepest setting works best for most carpets. Push down on the lever firmly to get a good stretch. You should feel the carpet stretch and see wrinkles disappear. Smaller spans require less pressure. If it takes all your strength to push down the lever, you're overstretching, and if it pushes down with little effort, the carpet isn't tight enough. To increase the force, lift the head free of the carpet, raise the handle, embed the head and try again.

Using a knee kicker

After stretching the length, use the knee kicker to set one side

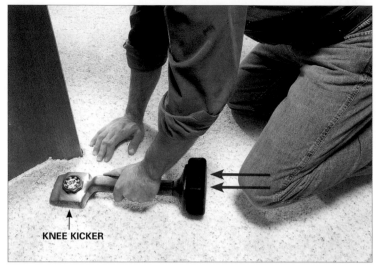

KNEE KICKER

9. Stretch any remaining tight areas with the knee kicker. Rest the teeth about 6 in. back from the wall or built-in and "kick" with the spot above your kneecap. Then embed the carpet with your hand.

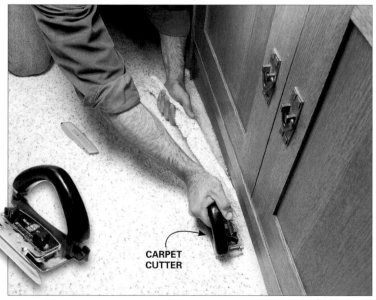

CARPET CUTTER

10. Hold the carpet cutter tight to the built-in (or baseboard) and cut through the front side of the carpet.

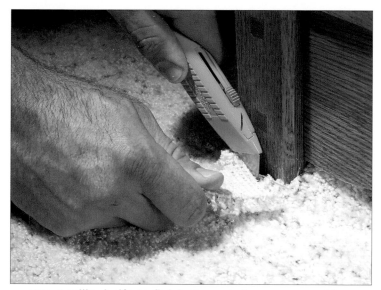

11. Use a utility knife to finish the cuts in corners and to trim around projections and other tight areas. Cut from the back side, leaving the carpet about 1/8 in. overlong to tuck tightly against the built-in.

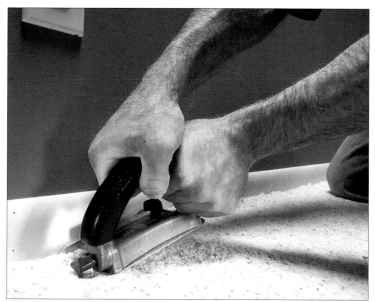

12. Embed the carpet edge firmly in the tack strip and under baseboards by forcing the front edge of the carpet cutter into the carpet and dragging it along the wall.

(the door side; Step 3, p. 67). Also use the knee kicker to stretch confined areas where the power stretcher won't fit (Step 4, p. 67). Set the teeth of the knee kicker into the carpet about 6 in. away from the wall and kick against it with the area above your kneecap (Photo 9). Immediately after kicking, embed the carpet in the tack strip with your hand to hold it in place. With more or harder kicks, you can "ratchet" the carpet tighter.

Using a carpet cutter

Using a carpet cutter and a utility knife (Photos 10 and 11), cut off the excess after the carpet is completely stretched. Cut an entry point for the cutter with the utility knife from the back. The cutter is designed to trap the carpet against the woodwork and cut it accurately. You'll have to push hard to force the carpet against the wood, otherwise you may cut it too short or long. If you don't cut enough, make another pass in both directions. If the rental store doesn't rent carpet cutters, you'll have to make all of your cuts with a utility knife, working from the back side. Be careful and work slowly to keep your cut accurate.

How to repair carpet

The carpet in your home is a big investment. So it's frustrating when a sputtering ember from the fireplace burns a hole in your beautiful rug or a spring storm floods the basement family room. But you don't have to call in a pro or just live with the damage until you replace the carpet. Solving these problems yourself isn't difficult, and you can increase the life of your carpet and save some real money.

Here is how to fix three common problems:

➤ Small damaged spots such as holes, tears or burns

➤ Wet carpet from leaks or flooding

➤ Carpet that has pulled out of a metal threshold

1 Patch a damaged spot

2 Rescue wet carpet

3 Reattach pulled-out carpet

Patch a damaged spot

You can patch a small hole, tear or burn using techniques that will make the repair virtually invisible. You'll need a small "plug" of carpet that matches the damaged piece. If you don't have a remnant, you can steal a piece from inside a closet or underneath a piece of furniture you never intend to move. (This may sound extreme, but it's a lot cheaper than replacing the entire carpet.)

If you have a "plush"-type carpet with a flat surface and no pattern, you can make a repair that's absolutely invisible. If your carpet has a color pattern, a textured surface design or looped yarn, you'll have to be fussier when you cut the plug, and the repair may be visible (but you're probably the only one who will notice it).

Before starting this repair, buy a carpet knife that has replaceable blades. You'll also need a roll of one-sided carpet tape. Be sure to choose heavy-duty tape reinforced with mesh, not the thin, flimsy version or the "hot-melt" type that requires a special iron to apply.

....

Cut out the damage and a matching plug

Be sure the area you're working in is well lit. To mark the area you'll cut out, part the carpet fibers around the damage as if you were parting your hair (Photo 1). Keep the part lines at least 1/2 in. from the damaged spot. Then cut along

1. Part the carpet fibers with a Phillips screwdriver. The parts mark your cutting lines and let you cut the backing without cutting or tearing the fibers.

2. Cut through the carpet backing. Make the cuts as straight as you can and avoid cutting completely through the carpet pad.

the parts using a sharp, new blade in your carpet knife (Photo 2).

Next, cut a replacement plug, using the cutout as a template. To start, make a first cut in the replacement material, using a straightedge to guide your carpet knife. Then set the cutout on the replacement material with one edge aligned along that first cut. When you lay the cutout on top of the replacement material, make sure their naps are running in the same direction. You can tell which direction the nap is running by rubbing your hand over the carpeting and watching which way the fibers fall or stand up. Once you have the cutout lined up correctly, part the fibers around the three uncut sides just as you did before.

Cut along the parts and test-fit the plug in the cutout hole, making sure the nap of the plug matches the nap of the surrounding carpet. If the plug is a little too big, trim off a single row of fibers with sharp scissors (old, dull scissors will tear the fibers).

A carpet knife makes straighter, cleaner cuts than a utility knife.

Prepare the hole for the new plug

Cut pieces of carpet tape and position them in the hole without removing the backing (Photo 3). Cut the ends of the tape diagonally so the pieces will frame the hole without overlapping. The tricky part is getting the tape positioned so it's halfway under the plug and halfway under the surrounding carpet. A helper makes this easier.

After marking their positions in the hole, remove the pieces from the hole, and carefully (this is sticky stuff!) remove the protective backing from the tape. While pulling the carpeting up with one hand, slip the tape pieces back into the prepared hole one piece at a time (Photo 4). Be sure the edges of the tape line up with your markings.

CARPET TAPE

3. Test-fit all the pieces of carpet tape before you stick them in place permanently. Mark a square on the carpet pad to help align each piece later.

4. Peel off the tape's backing and set each piece in place, sticky side up. Don't let the super-sticky tape touch the carpet backing—or anything else—until it's in position.

5. Set the plug tightly against one side of the hole. Then lower the other edges into place, holding back the surrounding fibers. Press the plug into the tape with your fingers, then with a carpet tractor.

Insert the plug

Now you're ready to fit the new plug into the hole. Pull the fibers of the surrounding carpet back from the edges. Push one side of the plug lightly onto the tape to make sure it's set exactly right—you really only have one shot at this (Photo 5). After you're sure the plug is placed correctly, use your fingers to work in the direction of the nap all the way around the hole as you press the plug down firmly onto each side of the tape.

A carpet tractor will do the best job of meshing the fibers, but a seam roller or even a rolling pin would work too. Place a heavy book on top of the plug overnight. Trim any fibers sticking up with sharp scissors. You'll be surprised how "invisible" this repair is once you're finished. You can vacuum and clean your carpeting as you normally would, and this repair should last as long as your carpet does.

A carpet tractor will mesh the fibers and make the repair invisible.

Rescue wet carpet

When carpet gets soaked, you have to act fast. The longer it stays soggy, the more likely it is to stretch out, discolor or get moldy. If a large area is waterlogged, complete replacement may be the best option. But if only a corner or a small room is soaked, you can save the carpet with just a couple of hours of work.

....

Tear out the soggy pad

First, go to the corner nearest the wet area, grab the carpet with pliers and pull the carpet off the tack strip. Continue pulling the carpet off the tack strip by hand until you can fold back the entire wet section. Run a fan or two to dry the carpet.

Wet carpet pad is like a big sponge. You have to get rid of it ASAP. Cut around the wet area with a utility knife. Make straight cuts so you have straight seams when you patch-in the new pad. If the pad is glued to a concrete floor, scrape it up with a floor scraper (Photo 1). If the pad is stapled to a wood subfloor, just pull up chunks of pad and pry or pull out the staples if you have just a few. For faster removal on a larger area, use a floor scraper. Have garbage bags handy to prevent drips on the carpeting. Wet pad is heavy. Don't fill the bags so full that you can't haul them out without wrecking your back!

Wipe up any water on the floor, then flop the wet carpet back into place. Drying it flat and in place helps the carpet retain its shape. Run fans until the floor and carpet are completely dry. This can take a couple of days.

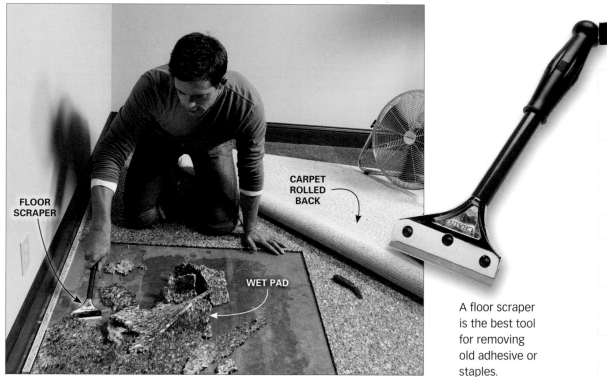

FLOOR SCRAPER

CARPET ROLLED BACK

WET PAD

A floor scraper is the best tool for removing old adhesive or staples.

1. Dry out wet carpet right away. Fold back the carpet and start a fan. Cut around the soaked section of pad and scrape it up.

Patch-in the new pad

Measure the area of pad you need to replace and take a piece of the old pad to a flooring store or home center to find similar replacement pad. The color doesn't matter, but the new pad must be the same thickness and density as the old pad. Some stores will cut the pad to the size you need.

Fasten the pad to a concrete floor with carpet pad adhesive and duct-tape the seams together (Photo 2). On a wood subfloor, all you need is a staple gun and 5/16-in. staples. Use a utility knife to trim off any pad covering the tack strip.

Reattach the carpet

As you refasten the carpet to the tack strip, you need to stretch it toward the wall. If you're dealing with a corner or a small area, you can use a knee kicker alone (see Photo 9, p. 68). Starting at one end of the loose carpet, set the head of the kicker about 2 in. from the tack strip and nudge the carpet tight against the wall. Force the carpet into the tack strip with a stiff putty knife. Also, tuck the edge of the carpet into the space between the wall and the tack strip with a putty knife. Continue along the wall, moving the kicker over a few inches each time.

If you're dealing with a larger area of carpet or if the carpet has stretched out of shape, bubbled or wrinkled after getting wet, you'll need to rent a power stretcher to restretch the carpet. For help with that job, check out the "stretching sequence" on p. 67.

CARPET PAD ADHESIVE

DUCT TAPE

NEW PAD

2. Lay replacement pad after the floor has dried. Duct-tape the seams where new pad meets old, and fasten the pad to the floor with adhesive or staples.

Reattach pulled-out carpet

If you have carpet that has pulled loose from a metal threshold, fix it now, before the exposed edge of the carpet begins to fray. If the damage extends more than an inch or so away from the threshold, you won't be able to make a good-looking repair. Aside from standard hand tools, you'll need a carpet knife and a knee kicker, which you can rent by the day at any rental center. You'll also need a new metal threshold and 1-1/2-in. ring-shank drywall nails.

Remove the old threshold

This repair is much easier if you first remove the door. You can do it with the door in place, but it'll take a little longer and you risk scratching the door. Carefully

THRESHOLD

1. Bend open the threshold's lip to release the carpet. Be careful not to snag the carpet as you push the screwdriver under the lip.

pry up the lip of the existing metal threshold along its entire length using a screwdriver or flat pry bar (Photo 1). Since you'll be replacing the threshold, you don't have to worry about wrecking it, but you want to work carefully so you don't damage the carpet edge even more. Once the threshold lip is bent up, use pliers to gently pull the carpeting up from the teeth inside the threshold. Roll the carpet back slightly to get it out of the way (you can leave the carpet pad in place).

Pry up the threshold slightly and pull the nails (Photo 2).

pro tips!

➤ To get an exact measurement for cutting the new threshold, don't measure the old threshold because it may be kinked. Instead, measure the opening and then cut the threshold with metal snips or a hacksaw.

2. Pry up the threshold just enough to raise the nail heads. Then pull the nails and remove the threshold. Work from the carpeted side to avoid scratching the hard flooring. Nail down a new threshold.

Install the new threshold

If the carpet edge is in good shape, you can place the new threshold exactly where the old one was. If the edge is badly frayed, you'll need to trim off the damage using a carpet knife and a straightedge. Then position the new threshold farther into the carpeted room to compensate for the width you trimmed off. In most cases, you can place the new threshold about 1 in. from the original position, but not more. If you've moved the threshold more than an inch, you may also need to trim the carpet pad so it doesn't cover the threshold pins.

If you're working on a wood subfloor, nail down the replacement threshold with 1-1/2-in. ring-shank drywall nails. On a concrete floor, use heavy-duty construction adhesive to glue the threshold to the floor, and allow a day for it to dry before moving on to the next step.

KNEE KICKER

3. Nudge the carpet toward the threshold with a rented "knee kicker" and force the carpet into the threshold's teeth with a stiff putty knife.

You can rent a knee kicker for a day at any tool rental center.

Attach the carpet

Now you're ready to attach the carpet to the new threshold. Starting at one end of the threshold, set the head of the knee kicker about 2 in. from the threshold and kick with your knee to stretch the carpet toward the threshold (Photo 3). Kick firmly, but not with all your strength or you might rip the carpet. Force the carpet into the threshold teeth with a stiff putty knife. Then move the kicker over a few inches (the width of the kicker's head) and repeat the process until you reach the other end of the threshold. When you're done, tuck any loose carpet under nearby baseboards with a stiff putty knife. Finally, pound down the threshold lip with a rubber mallet (Photo 4).

4. Drive down the lip, tapping gradually back and forth along its entire length. On the final pass, pound hard to lock the carpet into the threshold.

How to tear out old carpet

Having new carpet installed or switching from carpet to hardwood floors? Here's how to remove old carpet quickly and efficiently.

Before the tear-out

Talk with your trash hauler to see if they will accept rolled-up strips of carpet along with the regular trash. If not, some cities have carpet recycling programs or they may have suggestions for how to dispose of it.

Before you begin tearing up carpet, remove any doors that swing into the room, including bifold closet doors. Doors that swing into adjoining rooms can stay in place. Then clear the floor completely, removing all the furniture from the room. Slip on a pair of gloves to protect your knuckles from the abrasive carpet backing and the needle-sharp tack strip. There's a lot of dust trapped inside old carpet, so if you're sensitive to dust, strap on a dust mask, too.

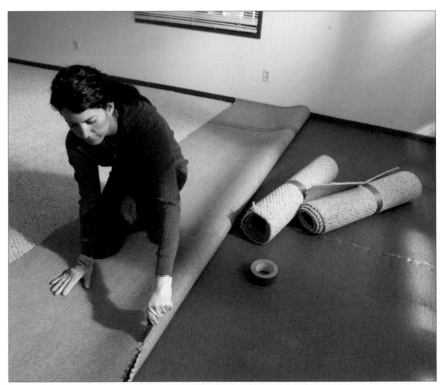

1. Fold the carpet over for easy cutting and slice it into narrow strips. Roll up the strips and tape them for easy handling.

Pull, cut and roll

To detach the carpet from the tack strip that holds the carpet in place along walls, start in a corner, and grab the carpet with pliers and pull. Then grab the carpet by hand and continue to pull it up along an entire wall. Fold back about 3 ft. of carpet and cut it into easy-to-handle strips (Photo 1). Carpet is much easier to cut from the back than from the front. Use a sharp new blade in your utility knife and be careful not to slice into the baseboard or walls.

Keep pulling back the carpet and slicing it into strips. When you come to a "transition" where the carpet meets another section of carpet or other flooring, cut the carpet and leave the transition in place (Photo 2). If you have a metal transition that's in good condition, the installer may decide to leave it in place. If the carpet is seamed to another section of carpet, the installer can separate the seam without damage to the carpet that's staying in place.

To remove carpet from stairs, start at the top. If there's a metal nosing at the top of the stairs, pry it up to remove it. If not, cut the carpet near the top of the top riser, grab the cut end and pull the carpet off the stairs by hand. Wear gloves to protect your hands from the staples that hold the carpet in place. Some stairs are covered with short sections of carpet that wrap over just one tread and riser. If you find yourself pulling up one long piece, slice off sections as you go to

2. Leave transitions alone. Cut the carpet a few inches from where it meets other flooring and let the installer tackle the transition work.

make pulling easier. When you've torn off all the carpet and pad, pull out all the staples with pliers.

Cut the pad into strips and roll it up just as you did with the carpet. On a concrete floor, the pad is glued in place, so big chunks of pad will remain stuck to the floor. To remove them, use a floor scraper. Some scrapers have razor-sharp blades; others have blunt blades. Either type works fine on concrete.

On a plywood or particleboard subfloor, you'll have hundreds of staples to deal with. You can pull staples with pliers, of course, but that can take hours. With a sharp-bladed floor scraper, the job takes just a few minutes (Photo 3). The blade will shear off some staples and

3. Get rid of carpet pad staples fast with a floor scraper. If the blade digs into the wood, scrape from a lower angle.

pro tips!

Carpet-scrap workbench protector

Don't scratch a picture or cabinet frame, or any other piece of woodwork, on a dinged up workbench. Next time you sand a project, lay down a scrap piece of carpet on the workbench. The carpet will protect the wood you're working on, keep it stationary as you sand and dampen the sander vibrations on your hands.

If you don't have any scrap carpet, a 2 x 6-ft. washable runner from a home center works great—just shake it out between jobs and roll it up for storage.

yank out others. Be sure to go over the whole floor so you don't leave any behind. If the scraper digs into the floor, flip it over so that the blade's beveled side faces down. If it still digs, work at a lower angle.

Trash the tack strip?

In most cases, you should leave the old tack strip in place, but there are a couple of exceptions: Remove any sections that are rotten, delaminating or badly rusted. Rust can "bleed" through the carpet, creating stains on the surface. You should also remove the tack strip if it's less than 1/4 in. from the baseboard. The installer needs a gap at least 1/4 in. wide to tuck the edge of the carpet down against the baseboard. To remove a tack strip, just pop it up with a flat pry bar. Tack strip is available at home centers.

Chapter **4**

Interior Wood Trim

Interior trim buying tips

Interior trim can add definition and refinement to a room, and wood remains a good choice for material. To get a pleasing result with wood, you need to carefully select the individual pieces of lumber at the store, paying attention to grain and color. Today, synthetic trims can sometimes be a better option. Here are a few tips to help you no matter which material you choose.

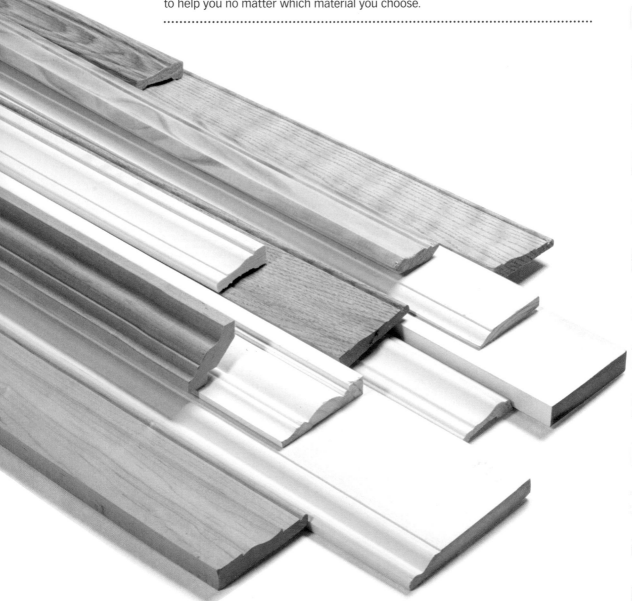

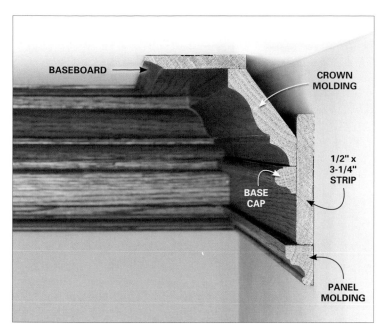

BASEBOARD →

CROWN MOLDING

BASE CAP

1/2" x 3-1/4" STRIP

PANEL MOLDING

Combine smaller molding to create large profiles

You can save money and hassles by buying separate pieces of trim and assembling them yourself rather than buying elaborate premilled moldings. Cutting, coping and fitting wide trim is tricky. If you mess up, you'll be wasting trim that can cost several dollars per foot. If possible, try to replicate the profile you're after by assembling the correct individual pieces yourself.

Bad

Good

Match the grain

Occasionally you'll need to splice trim pieces. If you're trimming with natural wood, that splice will stick out like a sore thumb if you're not careful. If you need to splice trim on long walls, spend extra time choosing those pieces to make sure the grain patterns match and the wood tones are similar. When the pieces are joined, the splice will be nearly invisible.

Buy primed trim if you're painting

This is a no-brainer. Primed trim speeds up the finishing process. It's easier to spot defects and nail holes on primed trim, so you can fill them before the final coats of paint. It's even simpler to cope primed trim because the contrast between the raw wood and the painted surface gives you a crisp profile line to follow. So don't buy raw wood if you're going to paint.

Get the longest pieces you can handle

Even if you need mostly short pieces, it's wise to buy the longest trim you can fit into your vehicle. Here's why:

> ➤ You'll have fewer splices and more one-piece trim lengths, which look much better than any splice ever would.

> ➤ You'll be able to pick and choose to closely match grains so they blend together.

> ➤ You'll have plenty of short lengths left over for smaller projects.

You can order rare moldings

No lumberyard or home center carries every molding profile made. Some styles are rare, especially in an older home. Even so, most are still made and available by special order. Take a short length of trim with you to the store and ask to see the profile chart. Any store that sells trim will have one. Match it to your sample and ask whether it can be ordered. It may be expensive, but you'll get the molding you want.

Avoid using MDF trim in moist places

MDF (medium-density fiberboard) is inexpensive and a great material for painted trim, but only if you're installing it in a permanently dry place. Installing it near the floor or near windows where water or condensation sometimes collects is a recipe for disaster. The MDF will soak up water like a sponge, expand and shed paint in very short order. So avoid using MDF anywhere at risk for getting wet.

How to stain wood trim

No matter how skillfully you install your trim work, it won't look good unless it has a fine finish. Uneven color, dust-flecked surfaces and brush marks all distract the eye and ruin the natural beauty of the wood. Yet achieving a smooth, flawless finish doesn't require expensive tools or special knowledge or skills.

Here we'll show you a simple three-day process that'll give you great results every time. We'll show you how and when to sand, using the correct sanding products. (It's not the tedious, mind-numbing job you might think it is!) Then we'll tell you how to apply stain evenly and without blotches on all the surfaces. Finally, we'll show you the best ways to get a smooth satiny surface with a sanding sealer and varnish.

We'll limit our staining techniques to methods that work well on coarse-grained woods, such as oak, ash and walnut. Achieving an even, blotch-free finish on fine-grained woods like cherry, maple, birch, pine and fir is much more difficult and requires extra steps we won't cover here.

Wood finishing isn't complicated, but it does require patience and attention to detail. It pays to get each step right the first time. Going back to correct mistakes is time consuming, and it's nearly impossible to achieve blemish-free results.

Choosing stain and finish

We recommend finishing your wood with oil-based stain (see "Test the Stains," p. 97) and varnish (alkyd) with a compatible sanding sealer beneath it. These finish types are the easiest to apply. Don't confuse alkyd varnishes with polyurethane ones. Polyurethane finishes are tough and have their place, especially on high-wear, water-prone surfaces like tabletops and hardwood floors. But they're less forgiving to use. Alkyd varnish, on the other hand, is easier to sand, which is an advantage if you have runs or drips or would like to apply a second topcoat.

You'll likely have two sheen choices—gloss (shiny) and satin (flat)—but don't be afraid to mix equal quantities of gloss and satin if semigloss is the look you're after. Few home centers carry alkyd varnishes, so you're better off shopping at a paint or woodworking supply store. Read the labels carefully: You'll find that just about every can on the shelf will be a urethane-type finish.

A sanding sealer is the perfect foundation for the varnish topcoat. It's formulated with more solids than conventional clear coats, making it very easy to sand. And varnish adheres better to a well-sanded, sealed surface. Pick a sealer that's designed for the overlying varnish, preferably of the same brand. If you use a sanding sealer that's incompatible with the varnish, the surface may crinkle or even flake off.

Begin by sanding

A good finish starts with sanding the bare wood with a 100-grit sanding sponge and/or paper. This step is crucial for achieving a uniform wood surface that'll absorb stain evenly. It also smooths out surface imperfections, which might show through the clear coat. Your goals are to eliminate the sawmill "burnish" (shiny surface left by the planer), smooth off any standing rough wood fibers and sand out any blemishes. Blemishes can include dirt, fingerprints, machining imperfections and label residue. Don't sand with finer grits at this stage or you're likely to end up with uneven stain.

Step 1: Sand

Step 2: Stain

Step 3: Seal

Step 4: Varnish

The sanding tool you select depends on the profile and size of the trim you're finishing. For large areas or deep imperfections like chatter marks (washboard textures) from the mill planers, use a random orbital sander. It's aggressive and cuts and smooths quickly.

For hand-sanding, use a sanding sponge for flat areas (Photo 1), a sanding pad for curves (Photo 2) and a folded piece of sandpaper for tight crevices (Photo 3). Always sand in the direction of the grain and sand every square inch whether you think it needs it or not. Your fingertips and eye will tell you when enough is enough. But look closely with good light before you call the job finished. Otherwise, imperfections like scratches caused by cross-grain sanding or chatter marks will become painfully

obvious when you start staining. Another common problem is burn marks. Sometimes extra elbow grease will be needed to eliminate those. This may sound like a lot of work, but, if you use fresh paper and sponges, the sanding goes fast.

Clean the room

A clean work area is crucial for a smooth, blemish-free finish. If you have the option, sand the wood outdoors or in a room that's separate from the finishing area.

If you're forced to sand in the finishing area, wait several hours after sanding before cleaning the room, to give the dust a chance to settle out of the air. Vacuum the floor and any nearby work surfaces. Then damp-mop those surfaces too. Avoid

100-GRIT SANDING SPONGE

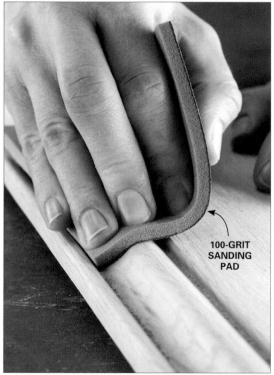

100-GRIT SANDING PAD

1. Sand flat surfaces with a 100-grit sanding sponge, in the direction of the grain, until you eliminate imperfections and rough areas.

2. Sand curves with a 100-grit pad. You can easily mold it to the contours of the various trim profiles.

sweeping—it just stirs up more dust. If there are rooms overhead, declare a moratorium on overhead foot traffic during finishing. Otherwise dust on the underside of the floor will rain down on wet finishes. Or do your clear-coat work after everyone's gone to bed. If you're working in a room that's heated or cooled with forced air, warm or cool the area a few hours ahead and then shut off the system until clear finishes are applied and become dry to the touch. That'll keep ventilation fans from stirring up more dust or bringing it in from other rooms.

Brush on the stain and wipe it off fast

The key to getting an evenly stained surface is to saturate the wood thoroughly and then wipe the stain off evenly. Start by stirring the stain. Scrape the stir stick across the bottom and pull up any settled solids, then work them into the solvent until they're all dissolved. (Use the same method to mix the sanding sealer and the varnish later.) The best application method is to simply dip a natural-bristle brush into the stain and brush it right onto the wood (Photo 4). Rags are messy and waste stain. Don't skimp when you're applying stain—more is better.

Wipe off the stain with clean cotton rags in the same order you put it on. The idea is to let it soak into all areas of the wood for about the same amount of time (Photo 5). Wipe with light, even pressure. You'll know if you wipe too lightly because you'll leave streaks. Refold wiping rags

100-GRIT SANDPAPER

3. Sand tight cracks with folded sandpaper. The edge will wear quickly, so refold the paper often.

2-1/2" CHINA-BRISTLE BRUSH

4. Saturate the wood with stain by brushing a liberal coat quickly over the entire surface.

frequently so you have dry cloth for most strokes, and grab a new rag whenever one gets soaked.

Next, "dry-brush" any cracks or crevices that the rag couldn't reach by dragging a dry brush through them (Photo 6). Wipe off the bristles on a rag or newspaper between strokes to keep the bristles dry and to avoid smearing. Don't waste time. It doesn't take long for stain to start drying, and it becomes sticky and hard to remove. If the stain gets tacky before you can wipe it off, simply apply more stain to soften it and then wipe it off again.

Finally, closely examine the surface for smudges, brush marks and blotches. Look for swirls left by rags and wipe them down again. These marks are easy to miss but you will see them after finishing, so examine the surface carefully.

If you spot areas in the finish that seem too light, add more stain. Let it sit for a couple of minutes and then wipe it off again. Work quickly; as the stain dries, it will smudge. Lighten dark areas by rubbing them lightly with a rag dampened with paint thinner. Make these color tune-ups for each piece right after staining. It's easiest to make color corrections while the stain is still damp. Let the stain dry overnight before you start the finish coats. If you're unhappy with grain lines that are too dark compared with the surrounding wood (Photo 5), restain and wipe the whole surface and let it sit overnight again.

COTTON RAG

GRAIN LINES

5. Wipe off the stain gently and evenly with clean cotton rags in the same order that the stain was applied. Watch for streaks.

DRY-BRUSH THE CRACKS

6. Clean stain from cracks and crevices with a dry brush. Wipe the brush on a clean rag or brush it on newspaper to clean off the stain between strokes. Let the stain dry overnight.

Brush on a sanding sealer

Brush on the sanding sealer in the direction of the grain until the whole surface is coated (Photo 7). Shine a strong light on the wet surface to highlight areas you might have missed (they'll be dull). Then add more finish wherever it's needed. Immediately "tip-off" the wet finish by stroking the entire surface from end to end with long, light, overlapping strokes of the wet brush (Photo 8). That'll further even out the coat and help eliminate brush marks. Work quickly; sanding sealers dry fast. If you wait too long before tipping off, you'll leave brush marks. If you see brush marks after tipping off, leave them and sand them out later. Lastly, look carefully at the edges to find any drips and smooth them out with the brush. Leave the wood lying flat during the finish application and while it dries afterward. That'll minimize runs and sags and help finishes to "level out" so brush marks will disappear.

Sand the sealer before varnishing

After the sealer dries, lightly sand the surfaces with 240- or 280-grit (extra-fine) sanding pads or paper. You'll know it's smooth enough when you see a fine dust on all the surfaces and they're smooth to the touch (Photo 9). The sanded surface should be uniformly dull. Shiny streaks or spots indicate missed spots.

7. Brush sanding sealer evenly onto the entire length of each board. Take care not to miss any spots.

LIGHT GRIP

8. "Tip-off" the surface immediately using long strokes from end to end. Let the sealer dry overnight.

Sand carefully, especially near sharp corners. It's easy to sand through the sealer and the stain to leave exposed raw wood. If that happens, just retouch with more stain to even up the color. There's no need to reseal small areas. Use a shop vacuum fitted with an upholstery brush to remove most of the dust. Remove the remaining dust by wiping the surfaces with a tack cloth (Photo 10).

Finish up with oil-based varnish

Brush on the varnish and tip it off with the same techniques you used for the sanding sealer (Photo 8). If you're working in a clean room and did a good job of sanding the sealer, one coat will be plenty.

Trim doesn't receive much wear or abrasion, so you don't need a tough, thick finish. But if you have dust specks, brush marks or other imperfections, don't try to pick them out of the wet finish. Let the finish dry overnight. If there are only a few specks, pick them out with your fingernail. If there are a lot of specks, resand and add another coat. Either way, specks in the finish mean the room is still dirty. Clean the room more thoroughly or find another, cleaner place to work for the next coat. To add another coat, prepare the surface as you did after the sanding sealer, including sanding the finish with extra-fine sanding grits, dusting the surfaces and wiping everything down with a tack cloth. Then add another topcoat of varnish.

9. Lightly sand the sealer with an extra-fine pad until the finish is smooth to the touch and a uniform flat, frosted color.

10. Vacuum most of the dust from the surface, then wipe off the remainder with a tack cloth. Then brush varnish over the entire surface, tipping it off to minimize brush marks.

Must-have finishing supplies

High-quality finishing supplies take the pain out of staining. Investing in these tools and accessories will greatly speed up the job and increase the quality of your finishing work.

➤ **Sanding supplies.** Buy 100-grit (medium) products for sanding the raw wood and either 240- or 280-grit (extra-fine) sanding paper, sponges and pads for sanding between clear coats, depending on the profiles you're sanding.

➤ **Brushes.** Buy two 2-1/2-in. china-bristle brushes (natural bristles). Use them for staining, dry-brushing (Photo 6) and applying the clear finishes. Don't spend less than $10 for a brush. (Pros will spend more than $20.) If you take care of it and clean it well, a top-quality brush will last for 20 years or more. A cheap brush is more likely to leave brush marks and bristles in the finish.

➤ **100-percent cotton painter's rags.** Buy a box at a home center for about $14. Don't use old bed sheets or clothes that contain synthetic fibers. They may leave behind dyes and won't absorb stain nearly as well.

➤ **Gloves.** A box of disposable gloves will protect your hands from solvents, and you won't have to struggle with putting on reusable ones after coffee breaks.

➤ **Mineral spirits.** Buy a 1-gallon can to clean brushes and to thin stain if needed.

➤ **Tack cloths.** Find tack cloths in the paint department. Use them to eliminate the last specks of dust after you sand between coats.

CHINA-BRISTLE BRUSHES

Test the stains

Oil stains are the finish of choice among pros because they're forgiving and easy to apply. Avoid "fast-drying" stains. You're better off with ones that require at least overnight drying time. Getting the best color usually requires stain mixing, so buy a few different 4-oz. cans in the color family you're interested in.

Then sand extra trim, cut it into 3-in. pieces and start experimenting. Mark all the pieces with the colors you use to keep them straight. You can lighten stain easily by diluting it with paint thinner. It's not unusual to use mixes that are 25 percent or even 50 percent paint thinner. But measure carefully so you can replicate your results on a larger scale. Next, finish the samples with the same sealer and varnish coats you plan to use, to get an accurate finished look.

Trying to match a stain that's on existing trim is difficult, especially if the trim is more than a few years old. Even pros rarely attempt it themselves. The best bet is to bring a sample of the finish you want to match, along with raw wood samples, to a paint store that offers a color-matching service. You may have to shop around a bit. As a last resort, find a furniture refinisher that's willing to help.

PROFESSIONAL
COST: $190,
per window

YOUR COST: $40,
per window

SAVINGS: $150
per window

COMPLEXITY
Moderate

TOOLS
Air compressor
Air hose
Brad nail gun
Caulk gun
Hammer
Miter saw
Safety glasses
Utility knife

MATERIALS
Trim
Wood glue
Shims

How to install window trim

When most pro carpenters install window trim, they don't even use a tape measure. Often, it's all done by eye, using a sharp pencil, a miter saw and an 18-gauge nailer. Here we'll show you how to pull off window trim installation that'll look every bit as good as a professional job—without hours of frustration. Shown here is standard trim, between 3/8 and1/2 in. thick—the types you'll find at any home center.

Step 1: Mark the length

Cut a 45-degree angle on one end of the trim and hold it so the short end of the angle overhangs halfway, or 3/8 in., onto the jamb. Then mark the other end flush with the inside of the jamb. That'll give you a 3/16-in. reveal.

Step 2: Get the spacing right

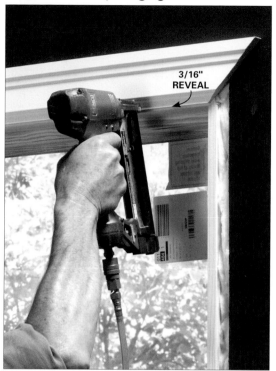

Hold the trim 3/16 in. away from the jamb at both ends and along the base of the trim. Nail the trim to the jamb with 1-in. brads spaced about every 6 in. Nail the thick part of the trim to the framing with 2-in. brads.

Step 3: Check the fit, then cut to length

Step 4: Glue and pin for a solid miter

GLUE SQUEEZE-OUT

Cut a 45-degree miter on one end of the trim board. Adjust the miter as needed for a perfect fit. Then scribe the cut length 3/16 in. past the bottom of the jamb. Nail the trim onto the jamb first and then to the framing, as you did with the top piece.

Glue and pin together the miter from both directions with 1-in. brads. Wipe the glue squeeze-out with a damp rag right away.

Step 5: Trim the other side

Repeat all the same steps on the other side of the window, fitting first the top miter, and then marking and cutting the bottom one. Nail the trim into place.

Step 6: Fit the first bottom miter

Cut an overly long piece of trim and cut a miter on one end. Overlap the far end to check the fit. Mark and recut the miter as needed for a perfect fit.

Step 7: Fit the opposite miter

Cut a test miter on the other end and check the fit. Adjust the miter as necessary until you're satisfied with the joint.

Step 8: Scribe for length

With the saw still set for the previous miter, flip the trim
over and scribe the length for the end that has that miter.
Transfer the mark to the front side and make the cut.

Dealing with problem drywall

If you have drywall that's "proud" (sticking out past the jamb) or recessed behind the jamb, you have to deal with it before trimming or the trim won't lie flat. Here's what to do:

If the drywall projects more than 1/8 in., crush in the drywall with a hammer. Just be sure the crushed area will be covered by trim. In this situation, your miters won't be 45 degrees. You may need to go as low as 44 degrees to get a tight miter.

If the drywall projects past the jamb 1/8 in. or less, and is close to the window jamb, just chamfer (bevel) the edge with a utility knife. Check to see if you've pared off enough drywall by holding a chunk of trim against the drywall and jamb. If it rocks and won't sit flush against both surfaces, carve out some more.

If the drywall's recessed behind the jamb, don't nail the trim to the framing at first. Only nail it to the jamb and pin the mitered corners together. After the window is trimmed, slide shims behind each nail location to hold out the trim while nailing, then cut off the shims. Caulk the perimeter of the trim to eliminate gaps before painting.

pro tips!

Here are six tips to help you avoid hassles:

➤ Whenever you can, cut with the thick side of the trim against the miter saw fence. You'll be less likely to tear out the narrow tapered edge that way.

➤ Cutting right up to the pencil mark almost always leaves pieces too long, so remove the pencil line with the blade. You'll most likely still have to shave off more.

➤ Sneak up on cuts by starting long and dipping the saw blade into the wood while you work your way to the cutoff mark.

➤ Trim out the biggest windows first. That way, you can reuse miscuts for the smaller windows and not run out of material.

➤ When nailing 3/4-in.-thick trim, use 15-gauge 2-1/2-in. nails for the framing and 18-gauge 2-in. brads for nailing to the jamb.

➤ To prevent splitting, avoid nailing closer than 2 in. from the ends.

Seamless miter trick

Here's a trick to make miters look great, but it only works if you're installing raw trim that will get finished after installation. It's easy. Glue the joint, then sand it smooth.

The sawdust from sanding will mix with the glue to fill any small gaps. Sanding the miter will also even out any slight level differences and make the job look more professional. Don't try to fill large gaps, especially in trim that'll be stained. Glue-filled gaps absorb stain differently than the surrounding wood and will stick out like a sore thumb.

1. Apply a thin layer of wood glue to the end grain of each piece before you assemble them. Use a damp (not wet) cloth to remove excess glue from the joint.

2. Sand over the miter with a small piece of 120-grit sandpaper. Sand across the joint and finish up by carefully sanding out any cross-grain sanding marks by moving the paper with the grain from both directions.

Wood trim drying rack

Have a whole bunch of trim to finish? This rack is easy to set up and takes up hardly any floor space—and it holds so much that you can finish all your trim at once.

All you do is pound 16d nails about 6 in. apart into 8-ft.-long 2x4s and screw the 2x4s to the wall. No open wall space? Clamp them to your garage door track. Just make sure you unplug the opener! There's your drying rack. Slather on the stain, varnish, paint, whatever—and then rest the pieces on the rack until they're dry.

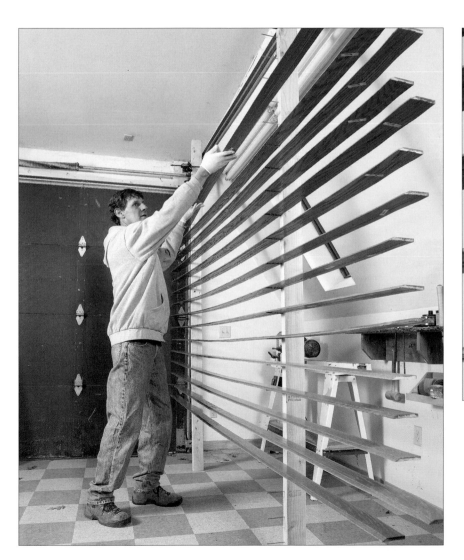

How to renew wood trim

Time takes a toll on woodwork. Moldings get dinged up, window stools lose their luster, and doors show the wear and tear of everyday use. But you can dramatically improve the appearance of stained and varnished woodwork without all the work and mess of a complete stripping and refinishing job. Gather the supplies in a 5-gallon bucket and tackle this wood trim renewal project one window or door at a time, whenever you have a few spare hours. Start in a corner or in an inconspicuous area — better to learn from your mistakes there than on the front door.

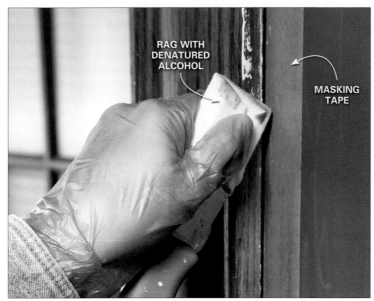

1. **Soften old paint along the edges of trim with alcohol.** A rag wrapped around a putty knife lets you scrub the trim without slopping alcohol onto the wall.

2. **Scrape away badly weathered finish.** A carbide paint scraper removes the old finish much faster than sandpaper. But be careful not to gouge the wood.

Start with a thorough cleaning

The first step in renewing your woodwork is cleaning it to remove grease and grime and create a contaminant-free surface for the new finish. Wash the woodwork with a TSP substitute. Use just enough cleaner to wet the surface. Scrub with a sponge dipped in the cleaning solution. Then rinse with a sponge and clear water and wipe off the wood with a dry rag.

If there's paint slopped onto the edges of your trim or spattered on the surface, now's the time to clean it off. A rag dampened with denatured alcohol will remove most paint spatters (Photo 1). Alcohol won't harm most finishes, but it will dissolve shellac. Don't worry if some of the finish comes off. You can touch it up later (Photo 7). Protect the walls with masking tape to prevent the alcohol from damaging the paint. For tougher paint spatters, use a fine synthetic abrasive pad (such as a 3M Wood Finishing Pad) dipped in denatured alcohol.

Scrape and sand badly damaged areas

Window stools and other areas exposed to moisture and sunlight may need to be completely refinished. In spots such as these where the wood is discolored and the finish worn away, you'll get the best results by scraping and sanding to expose bare wood (Photos 2 and 4).

If the wood has dark water stains that scraping and sanding won't remove, you can remove them with oxalic acid (Photo 3). Caution: Wear protective gear, including goggles, rubber gloves and a long-sleeve shirt, when you work with oxalic acid. Mix the oxalic acid in a plastic container. Add 1 oz. of oxalic acid powder (about 2 tablespoons) to 1 cup of hot water and stir it until the powder dissolves. Then brush the solution onto the stain with a disposable sponge brush and let it work for 20 minutes. You can repeat the process to further lighten the stain. Wipe the bleached wood with a sponge and clear water. Then neutralize the oxalic acid by applying a solution of 3 tablespoons of borax to 1 gallon of water with a sponge. Finally, rinse the bleached wood with water again and let it dry overnight. Then sand it with 120-grit followed by 180-grit sandpaper (Photo 4) and stain it to match the rest of the woodwork.

OXALIC ACID SOLUTION

WATER STAINS

3. **Bleach away deep stains that scraping or sanding won't remove.** You don't have to scrub; just let the oxalic acid penetrate and lighten the stain.

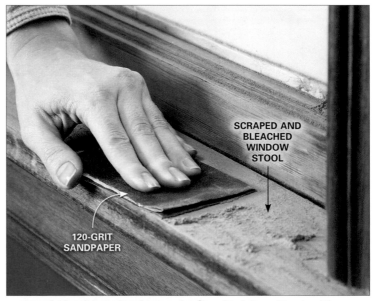

SCRAPED AND BLEACHED WINDOW STOOL

120-GRIT SANDPAPER

4. **Sand the bleached wood after it dries.** Start with 120-grit sandpaper. Then sand with 180-grit. Vacuum the dust before staining and finishing.

SCRUBBED
MOLDING

SYNTHETIC
FINISHING
PAD

5. **Rub the wood with an abrasive pad to create a slightly roughened surface for the new finish.** Vacuum the dust from the surface before wiping on a new coat of finish.

Fill small holes with wood putty

To make new finishes stick well, slightly roughen the old finish first (Photo 5). Synthetic finishing pads are the best choice because they conform to profiles and aren't as aggressive as sandpaper. Buy medium and fine and experiment in an inconspicuous area. Use the pad that roughens the finish without removing any stain.

Fill holes left by nails or screws with soft wood putty. Wood putty is available in many colors that you can blend for a perfect match. Application is easy. You just push it into the hole and wipe it off (Photo 6). There's no sanding required. Buy several shades of putty, ranging from dark to light, that are similar to the color of your trim. Then mix them to match the wood surrounding the hole. Push the putty into the hole and wipe off the excess with your fingertip. Then remove residue from around the hole by wiping over it with a clean rag. If your woodwork has filled nail holes that have darkened and no longer match, pick the old filler out and replace it with soft putty. Buy water-based putty if you plan to use water-based polyurethane.

WOOD PUTTY

SOFT PUTTY FILLER

6. Fill holes with perfectly matched putty. Just knead different colors together until you get an exact match.

Apply stain to hide dings and scratches

Completely refinishing the area may be the only way to make flawless repairs to badly damaged doors, windows and moldings. But you can greatly improve the overall appearance of worn or damaged wood with less drastic measures.

Disguise large areas where the stain is worn away by dabbing stain over the light areas to blend them in. The patched area may not match exactly, but at least the spot will be less obvious. Or simply wipe the surface of the wood with a rag dipped in stain to fill in small scratches and imperfections—you'll see a big improvement (Photo 7). Wipe the stain on. Then wipe off the excess with a clean rag. Allow the stain to dry overnight before you apply the finish.

One of the trickiest parts of a wood restoration project is finding stain to match. You can pry off a small piece of trim and ask the paint department to mix stain to match. Some paint stores and home centers offer inexpensive sample packets of stain. You can choose several samples that are close to the color of your wood and experiment in a hidden area to find the best color match. Then

SCRATCHED FINISH

MATCHING STAIN

STAIN RAG

RESTAINED AREA

7. Hide scratches, chips and worn-away finish with a fresh dose of stain. Then wipe the woodwork with a clean rag to remove the excess stain. Let the stain dry overnight.

buy a larger container. Another approach is to buy two or three cans of stain that are close to the color of your woodwork and mix them to get the right color. Use an eyedropper and disposable plastic cups to mix small batches until you get the proportions right. Keep notes so you can reproduce the results in a larger batch.

Refresh the finish

The final step in your trim renewal project is to apply a fresh coat of finish. Wipe-on polyurethane is a good choice because it's fast and easy to apply. You simply wipe it on with a soft rag and let it dry. Each coat is very thin and dries quickly. You can recoat in two or three hours if you want a thicker finish for extra protection. Several coats of wipe-on polyurethane are required to equal the thickness of one coat of brushed-on varnish, but it's easier to get a smooth, drip-free finish with wipe-on poly.

Fold a cotton rag to create a pad. Then dip an edge of the pad into a container of wipe-on polyurethane and press it against the side to wring out the excess. Wipe the polyurethane onto the wood in long strokes in the direction of the wood grain as you would if you were using a brush.

For window stools or other trim exposed to sunlight, consider using spar varnish. Spar varnish has built-in ultraviolet protection and is more flexible, so it holds up better in areas exposed to sunlight and water. Experiment on a scrap of trim or in an inconspicuous area to see if the slightly amber tint darkens the color too much.

When you've completed all of these steps, your woodwork will look like new and be protected by a fresh layer of finish. If you don't have time to do an entire room from beginning to end, just tackle one door or window whenever you have a few spare hours. You'll be done with a room before you know it.

Round up your supplies

Here we've listed the essential supplies you'll need for a basic wood renewal project and some optional materials and supplies you may need if you're refinishing window stools or removing stains. Most of the tools and supplies are available at paint stores, full-service hardware stores and home centers. Visit an art supply store for the artists' markers. Oxalic acid is available online at rockler.com or at woodworking stores and some hardware stores and lumberyards.

8. Restore the shine with a fresh coat of polyurethane. Wipe-on poly gives you a faster, smoother finish with less mess than brush-on poly.

Supplies you'll need:
➤ TSP-PF (phosphate free)
➤ Fine synthetic abrasive pads
➤ Denatured alcohol
➤ Disposable gloves
➤ Safety glasses
➤ Stain to match
➤ Wood putty to match
➤ Wipe-on polyurethane for varnished wood
➤ Rags
➤ Mineral spirits

Optional tools and materials:
➤ Paint scraper
➤ Oxalic acid
➤ Sandpaper
➤ Wood filler
➤ Felt-tip artists' markers
➤ Goggles
➤ Rubber gloves
➤ Spar varnish for window stools

Faux wood patch

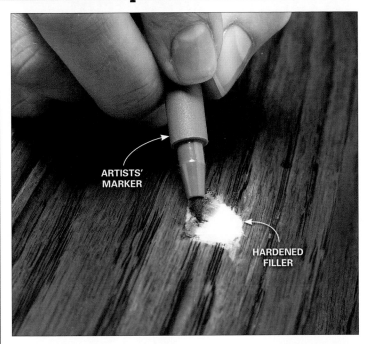

ARTISTS' MARKER

HARDENED FILLER

Dings and dents too large to fill with soft putty present a unique challenge. If you can't replace the wood, the next best thing is to patch the damage with filler and color the patch to match. Use hardening-type filler like Durham's Rock Hard Water Putty. Apply the filler carefully with as little excess as possible to minimize sanding. Let the filler dry and sand it smooth, being careful to avoid sanding away the finish on the surrounding wood. Then use felt tip artists' markers to "paint" the patch to match (see photos). Art supply stores are the best source of markers—you'll find endless shades of brown. Most other stores carry only one or two. The repair won't be perfect, but you may be surprised by how inconspicuous it is from a distance.

DARKER MARKER

FAUX WOOD GRAIN

PROFESSIONAL
COST: $100

YOUR COST: $0

SAVINGS: $100

COMPLEXITY
Simple

TOOLS
Utility knife
3-in. putty knives
Pry bar
Nippers

MATERIALS
None

How to remove wood trim

It can be difficult to remove wood trim without wrecking the walls or cracking the trim. This method gives you your best chance at removing the trim without damaging the wall or the wood.

1. Jam a pry bar between two knives and twist sideways.

Begin by cutting through any dried paint along the top edge of the trim with a utility knife. Then search for the filled nail holes at one end of the trim. Prying near those will keep you from breaking out the drywall. Slide a flexible 3-in. putty knife behind the trim and pry out slightly. With the knife in place, wedge in a pry bar and pry the trim out an inch. If it seems like the trim is about to crack, insert a second putty knife between the pry bar and the trim. Move to the next stud and repeat the procedure. Continue prying out the trim a little at a time down its length. Then go back to the beginning and pull the trim off.

Pushing the nails back through the front of the trim will splinter the wood. Instead, pull them through the back with nippers. Use just enough pressure to pull the nails to avoid cutting them off. If one breaks off, cut it as close as possible to the wood and leave it. That nub will just bury itself in the drywall when you reinstall it.

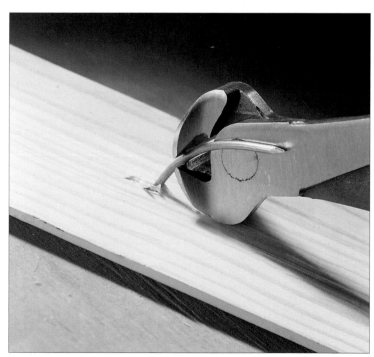

2. Grab the nail shaft near the wood with a pair of nippers. Roll the tool head against the wood to pull the nail out the back side of the trim.

Chapter 5

Saturday Morning Fixes

PROFESSIONAL
COST: $400

YOUR COST: $150

SAVINGS: $250

COMPLEXITY
Simple

TOOLS
Screwdriver
Circular saw
Clamps
Drill
Level
Miter saw
Utility knife
Rags

MATERIALS
Plywood
Back plates
Brad nails
Door bumpers
Drawer slides
Door and drawer
  catches
Toothpicks
Wood glue

Fix kitchen cabinets

Some cabinet fixes are tough, even for pros. But the most common problems are straightforward and perfect for beginners. Hit the hardware store in the morning to pick up supplies, then come home, get to work and you'll be done in time to make dinner (or order in!).

These fixes won't help with major problems like split panels on doors, but they will solve the little problems that bug you daily. Your cabinets will look and operate better—and sometimes a little satisfaction goes a long way.

NEW SLIDES

Replace worn-out drawer slides

Lubricants won't fix damaged drawer slides. They have to be replaced. This is a common problem on silverware drawers and other drawers that carry a lot of weight. Buy new slides that are the same, or nearly the same, as your old ones. Then it's just a matter of swapping them out. You'll find a limited selection of drawer slides at home centers, but there are dozens of online sources. Three sites are knobs4less.com, thehardwarehut.com and grainger.com. These sites also sell the plastic mounting sockets that attach to the back of the cabinet to hold the slides in place.

Build a shelf that won't sag

Don't bother replacing a sagging shelf with another 1/2-in.-thick shelf or it'll end up sagging too. Instead, cut a new shelf from 3/4-in. plywood. Make it the same length and 1-1/2 in. narrower (so you can add rails). Then glue and brad nail (or clamp) 1x2 rails along the front and back of the shelf, flush with the ends. The rails give the shelf additional support so it won't sag, even if you load it up with heavy cookware. Apply a polyurethane (or other) finish to match your other shelves.

3/4" PLYWOOD

1x2 LUMBER

Adjust Euro hinges

Adjusting cabinet doors with European hinges is as easy as turning a screw or two. Hinges like this one adjust in three directions; others adjust in two. If your door is crooked—not square with the cabinet—fix that first, then raise or lower it to the same height as adjacent doors.

For crooked doors, adjust the side screw on one hinge, which moves the door from side to side. It's a trial-and-error process. Make a small adjustment, then close the door to check its position. If the door is higher or lower than adjacent doors, loosen the mounting screws on both hinges, raise or lower the door, then tighten the screws. Place a straightedge across the door top or bottom to make sure it's level with neighboring doors.

If the door sticks out too far from the cabinet or the hinge side brushes against the cabinet when you open the door, adjust the depth screw. Some hinges move the door as you turn the depth screw; others require you to tap the door in or out and then tighten the screw.

Door adjustments aren't as easy if you have traditional hinges. If your doors are sagging, first try tightening the screws. If the hinges are bent, replace them if you can find a match.

MOUNTING SCREW

DEPTH SCREW

SIDE SCREW

Silence banging doors with bumpers

Doors and drawers slam loudly when wood smacks against wood. That's why most have "bumpers" near the interior corners to cushion the impact and reduce the noise. But the bumpers sometimes fall off (or kids pick them off). Get new ones at a home center. Peel off the backing and stick the bumpers in place. They're available clear or with felt, and in different thicknesses. Use bumpers of the same thickness as those on adjacent doors.

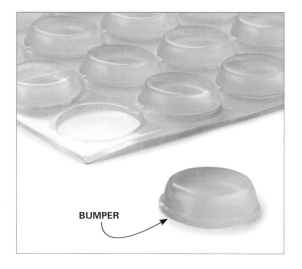

BUMPER

Fill in stripped screw holes

When the screws in your hinges or drawer slides turn but don't tighten, the screw hole is stripped. That can prevent doors and drawers from closing properly. Fix the problem with glue and toothpicks. Start by removing the hardware. Then apply a drop of wood glue to the ends of toothpicks and cram as many as will fit into the hole (maybe only two or three). Wipe away any glue that drips out. Let the glue dry, then use a utility knife to cut the toothpicks flush with the cabinet or drawer. Reinstall the hardware, driving the screw through the filled hole.

Beef up wimpy drawer bottoms

The thin plywood used for drawer bottoms sometimes gets wavy. Stiffen up the bottoms with 1/4-in. or 3/8-in. plywood. Cut the plywood to fit over the drawer bottom, leaving about a 1/4-in. gap on each side. Apply wood glue on the drawer bottom and set the plywood over it. Set a gallon or two of paint over the plywood to hold it in place until the glue dries.

Renew the shine

Grease splatters and smoke can leave a film on your cabinets, dulling the finish. Wash the cabinets with a wood cleaner to bring back the luster. Murphy Oil Soap is one type of cleaner.

Use a sponge to rub the cleaner onto the cabinets. Cleaners like Murphy's don't need to be rinsed off, which cuts your cleaning time. For stubborn grease spots, scrub lightly with the cleaner using a No. 0000 steel wool pad. Cleaning the cabinets once a year keeps them shiny and protects the finish.

Add back plates to cover worn areas

Years of opening doors and drawers can wear away the finish near cabinet knobs. Instead of undertaking the time-consuming task of refinishing the cabinets, try this quick fix: Install back plates under the knobs or handles. Simply unscrew the knob or handle, slide the back plate under it, then reattach the knob or handle. Back plates start at $2 and are available in a wide range of styles. You can special-order them at home centers or buy them online.

Two sources are knobs4less.com and amerockforless.com. They are also available at home centers.

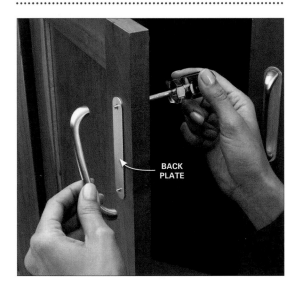

BACK PLATE

BACK PLATE

Repair busted drawers

Some drawers are held together by only a few drops of glue or short brad nails. When you first notice a drawer corner coming apart, take out the drawer and fix it. And if one corner is failing, others probably will too. Save yourself future hassles by repairing all the weak corners now. Place a piece of scrap wood against a corner and lightly rap it once with a hammer. If the corner comes apart, fix it. If not, it should hold up.

To fix the corner, first remove the drawer front, if possible. Most fronts are attached by screws driven from inside the drawer. Remove any fasteners from the corner, then scrape away the old glue with a utility knife. Reglue the corner, tap the sides back together and clamp the drawer until the glue dries.

Glue loose knobs

Once knobs fall off your cabinets, twisting them back on won't solve the problem. They'll just keep coming loose. Use a dab of thread adhesive to keep them in place. Apply the adhesive to the screw, then attach the knob. If you decide to replace the knob later, don't worry. You can remove it with a screwdriver.

GLUE

THREAD ADHESIVE

Lubricate sticking drawers

The fix for sticking drawers is easy. First remove the drawer. Wipe the drawer slides and the cabinet track with a clean cloth to remove any debris. Then spray a dry lubricant directly on the drawer slides. An 11-oz. can costs $7 at home centers; it'll say "dry lubricant" on the label. Replace the drawer and slide it in and out of the cabinet several times until it glides easily. If the drawer is still hard to open, replace the drawer slides (see p. 121).

Dry lubricants won't leave an oily residue that attracts dirt and dust. These lubricants also work great on squeaky hinges.

Pull doors shut with magnets

This trick is not new, but it still works. When your cabinet door is warped and won't fully close, simply install a magnetic catch at the problem area. Screw the magnetic catch to the cabinet rail or stile and the plate to the door. The magnet pulls the door closed. For powerful magnets, visit rockler.com and search for "magnetic catch."

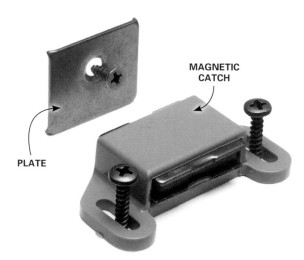

MAGNETIC CATCH

PLATE

Fill in scratches

Use a wood fill stick to make scratches less visible. The stick fills in and colors over the scratch. Soften the stick with a hair dryer to make the application easier. Then run the stick over the scratch and wipe away any excess with a cloth. The fill probably won't be an exact match with the surrounding cabinet, but it'll be close. The sticks work on shallow and deep scratches. They're available at home centers and online.

SCRATCH

FILL
STICK

Replace bad latches

Older cabinets sometimes have "roller catches" that hold the doors closed. If you have these and your door won't close or stay closed, loosen the screws to slide the catch forward or backward on the cabinet frame. Or replace it if it's broken. The catches are available at home centers for a couple of dollars.

Repair car dents

PROFESSIONAL COST: $200

YOUR COST: $30

SAVINGS: $170

COMPLEXITY
Easy

TOOLS
Drill
Rags
Tack cloth

MATERIALS
24-grit sanding wheel
80-, 180-, and 320-
   grit sandpaper
Plastic spreaders
Finishing glaze
Body filler
Wax remover

We've patched quite a few vehicle dents over the years and we usually did it the same way we tape drywall—by applying 5 lbs. of body filler and then sanding off 4.9 lbs. Then we went to "boot camp" at 3M and learned there's an easier way (as in, the correct way) to do dent repairs.

We asked 3M expert Jenn Cook to walk you through the same repair process. If you follow these steps, you can patch a dent yourself in just a few hours and save a few hundred bucks over body shop prices. Once the dent is patched, you just spray on a primer coat and matching paint from the dealer or an auto parts store. The repair won't look like a professional job, but at least it won't stand out like a sore thumb. Here's the process.

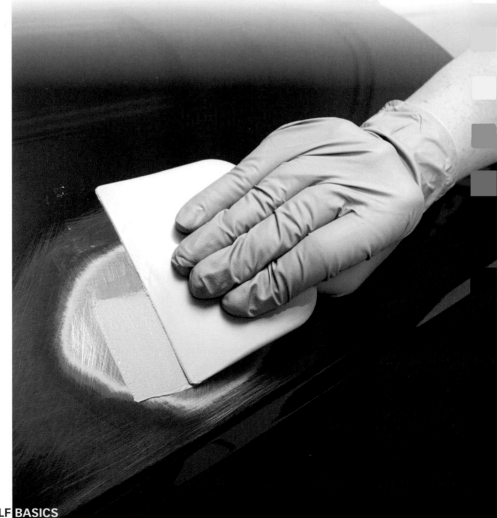

Pick up supplies

Stop at any auto parts store and buy a 24-grit sanding wheel and sheets of 80-, 180- and 320-grit sandpaper. Also buy a bottle of wax remover, a tack cloth, a mixing board, several plastic spreaders and a tube of finishing glaze.

Finally, you'll need body filler. Professional-grade filler is creamier and easier to spread and sand than bargain-priced products, so it's worth the extra cost.

Prep and clean before filling

Start by removing the paint inside and around the dent with 24-grit paper (Photo 1). Switch to 80-grit sandpaper and hand-sand the entire dent. Use the same sandpaper to rough up and feather the paint around the edges of the dent. Clean the entire area with wax remover and a clean rag. Then wipe with a tack cloth.

1. Remove the paint. Chuck the 24-grit disc into your drill and spin it deep into the dent, getting all the way down to the metal. Then work your way out to the edges.

Mix the filler

Don't mix body filler on a scrap piece of cardboard. Instead, use a mixing board or an old, clean cookie sheet you're willing to toss.

Scoop filler onto the mixing board and apply the hardener according to the directions. Then mix it using a spread-and-fold motion (Photo 2). The spreading and folding technique fully mixes the hardener into the filler and prevents air bubbles from forming. Never stir the mixture.

Apply the filler

Spread the filler to form a "tight" coat (Photo 3). That will burp air out of the scratches and wet the bare metal. Then apply a fill coat (Photo 4).

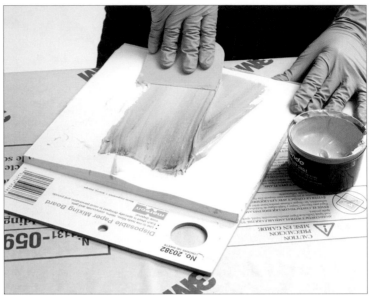

2. Spread, scoop and fold. Spread the filler down the mixing board in an S-shaped curve. Then scoop it up and fold it over. Repeat until the filler has a consistent color.

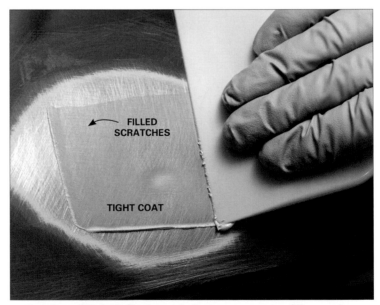

FILLED SCRATCHES

TIGHT COAT

3. Apply a "tight" first coat. Scoop up some filler and press it hard into the rough metal.

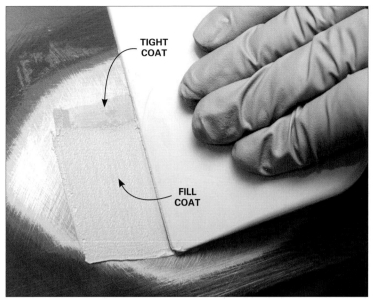

TIGHT COAT

FILL COAT

Sand to shape and glaze

Sand the filler to match the contours of the car body using 80- and 180-grit sandpaper. Then feather the edges of the filler right up to the painted edge.

Next, apply finishing glaze to the entire patch and then sand with 180-grit and then 320-grit sandpaper (Photo 5). Spray the patch with primer, and then paint it.

4. **Add more filler.** Wipe on a thicker layer of filler to completely fill the dent.

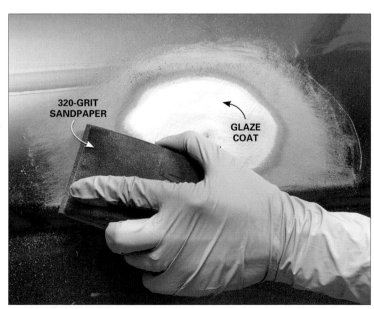

320-GRIT SANDPAPER

GLAZE COAT

5. **Sand the glaze.** Hand-sand the glaze coat with 180-grit and then 320-grit sandpaper to get a smooth finish. Then prime and paint.

Seal an asphalt driveway

An asphalt driveway can last almost 30 years. But you can't achieve that long life span unless the driveway was installed properly and you perform regular maintenance, like filling cracks annually and applying sealer when needed. To learn about filling the cracks, visit familyhandyman.com and search "fill asphalt cracks." Here we'll show you how to clean and prepare the driveway so you get the longest life and best protection from driveway sealer.

Preparation can take a full day (including drying time), and it's tedious. The application phase is much faster, taking only a few hours per coat for a typical driveway. Most sealer manufacturers recommend two coats with a minimum drying time of eight hours between coats, so this project will fill an entire weekend.

The materials cost about $100, but you'll save about $200 in labor over a professional job. A power washer speeds the cleaning process, but you can do the job without it. In addition to a squeegee or application brush, you'll need a broom, drill, mixing paddle, duct tape, dashing brush and poly sheeting to protect painted surfaces.

Buying the right materials

Driveway sealer is available in various grades and price ranges, from as little as $15 per approximately 5-gallon pail to about $35 per pail for a premium product. Some bargain products contain almost 50 percent water and have lower coverage rates and a correspondingly shorter guarantee, so they're not the most cost-effective solution over the long term. Use one of them if you're trying to spiff up the driveway before selling your home. Premium products, on the other hand, are made with higher-quality resins and UV stabilizers and contain filler and elastomeric material, so they last longer and carry a longer guarantee.

Manufacturers also make different formulas for different driveway conditions: one formula for newer driveways in good condition and another formula for older driveways that haven't been well maintained. The two formulas also vary in their coverage, so read the labels carefully and choose the correct sealer and quantity for your particular driveway. Follow the manufacturer's directions for the

Avoid these common driveway-sealing mistakes

➤ Depending on the sealer to fill cracks. It won't. Fill them properly before applying sealer.

➤ Failure to clean and prep the driveway before applying the sealer. If you don't want to spend time cleaning the driveway, you may as well skip the sealer too, because it won't stick to a dirty driveway.

➤ Failure to stir properly. Don't depend on a stir stick. It simply won't blend the water and solids enough to get a consistent mixture.

➤ Use of the wrong applicator. Using a brush when the manufacturer specifies a squeegee (or vice versa) will cause premature sealer failure.

➤ Applying sealer too often. Too much sealer will flake off. Wait until you begin to see asphalt aggregate before you apply a new coat of sealer.

1. **Soap and scrub.** Use the soap nozzle on your power washer or a garden hose applicator to apply the driveway cleaner. Then scrub the entire driveway with a stiff-bristle push broom.

type of applicator to use (brush or squeegee). Using the wrong one can cause premature failure.

You'll also need liquid driveway cleaner/degreaser to remove oil and tree sap. If your driveway has visible oil stains, pick up a bottle of oil spot primer.

Check the weather before you start

You'll need at least two days of dry weather to seal your driveway. Temperatures must be above 50 degrees F during application and throughout the night. And, it's best to avoid scorching-hot sunny days (the sealer may dry too fast). If you ignore the weather forecast, you may see $100 worth of sealer wash away in a heavy rain.

Start with cleaning and priming

Even if you think your driveway is clean, trust us, it isn't. Exhaust gas contains combustion byproducts that deposit a light, sometimes oily film on your driveway. That film, along with dirt and tree sap, must come off if you want the sealer to stick. So clean the driveway first (Photo 1).

Next, rinse the driveway with clear water (Photo 2). Let the driveway dry completely before applying the sealer. Then perform a final sweep with a push broom. Treat any oil stains with an oil spot primer (Photo 3).

2. Rinse with a strong stream. Flush the soap and dirt residue with a 40-degree power washer nozzle or a strong stream of water from your garden hose.

3. Pretreat the oil stains. Pour the oil spot primer on the damaged areas and brush it into the pores with a disposable chip brush. Apply a second coat to heavier stains. Let the primer dry fully before applying the driveway sealer.

Mask, stir, and trim

Driveway sealer will splash onto your garage door and sidewalks as you pour it. And it'll get all over your shoes and clothes. It's very difficult (often impossible) to remove later, so wear old work clothes and shoes. Mask the garage door with poly sheeting and apply strips of duct tape to concrete walks that butt up to the asphalt.

Choose an area on the driveway for mixing and cover it with poly sheeting to protect against spills (dried spills will show through the sealer). Remove the pail lids and cut a small hole in the center of one lid. Use that lid to prevent splashing during mixing. Stir until the mixture is smooth (Photo 4).

Next, cut in all four edges of the driveway with a large dashing brush (Photo 5). Clean the brush with soap and water as soon as you're done cutting in the edges—you'll need it again the following day. Then stage the pails equally down the driveway (Photo 6).

4. **Mix the sealer.** Start the mixing paddle near the top of the pail and slowly lower it into the contents settled at the bottom. Cycle the mixing paddle up and down while it spins to combine the water and solids into a smooth consistency.

5. **Cut in the edges.** Dip the dashing brush into the sealer and apply a liberal coating to all four edges of the driveway. Don't spread it too thin; you want it to fill in all the pores.

Pour and spread

Pour the sealer onto the driveway (Photo 7). Then spread the puddle with a squeegee or broom, depending on the manufacturer's directions (Photo 8). Pour enough sealer to maintain a puddle in front of the applicator tool.

When you reach the bottom of the driveway, cap the remaining pails and clean the squeegee or brush. Set the empty pails along the curb to prevent cars from ruining the job. Then let the sealer dry overnight.

Repeat the sealer application the next day. Let the sealer dry for 48 hours before driving on it (better safe than sorry). Don't ask how we learned that lesson.

POLY SHEETING TO MASK DOOR

STAGED PAILS

6. Stage the pails. Guesstimate the coverage of each pail and stage each additional pail along the driveway. That saves time and reduces the need to walk through wet sealer to get the next pail.

7. Pour onto the driveway. Start at the top left or right edge of the driveway and pour the sealer in an upside-down U-shape pattern.

8. **Spread the sealer.** Start at one leg of the upside-down "U" and apply even pressure to spread the puddle across the driveway and down along the opposite leg. Then pick up the excess sealer on the down leg and start the next row.

Driveway sealers: Real protection or just black paint?

Some asphalt driveway companies tell their customers that driveway sealer is a waste of money, that it's cosmetic and doesn't do anything to extend the life of the asphalt.

It's true that driveway sealer can't replace the liquid asphalt (oil/tar) that oxidizes and bakes out of the mixture from heat and sun exposure. But a high-quality sealer can dramatically reduce future heat and UV damage. Plus, it seals the pores to prevent aggregate breakup damage caused by water penetration, freeze/thaw cycles and chemicals. So it really does extend the life of your driveway.

PROFESSIONAL
COST: $170

YOUR COST: $20

SAVINGS: $150

COMPLEXITY
Moderate

TOOLS
Drill and bits
Hammer
Level
Miter saw
Nail set
Router and cove bit
Stud finder

MATERIALS
Finish screws
Wood glue
1x6 board

Fix a loose handrail

Whether you need to add a new handrail or firm up a wobbly one, here's a new handrail hanging method that's easy and super strong. The trick is to mount the handrail to a board first and then screw the board to the wall. This eliminates the hassle of trying to line up the brackets with the studs, and allows you to securely attach the end returns with screws running through the back side of the board. This method is much easier since most of the work is done on your workbench. And it also hides any damage from a poorly hung existing rail.

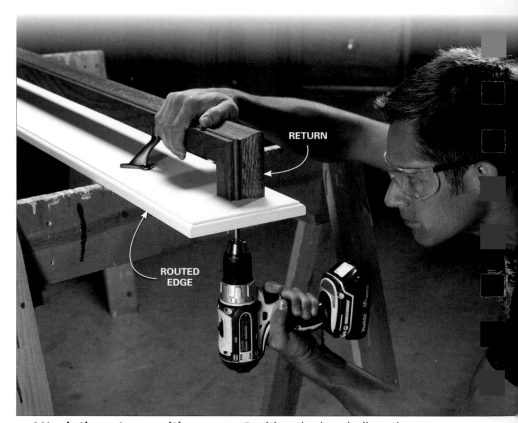

RETURN

ROUTED EDGE

1. **Attach the returns with screws.** Position the handrail on the board so the space above the rail and below the brackets is about the same, spacing the rail evenly from both ends. Drill pilot and countersink holes and screw through the board into the returns with 2-in. screws.

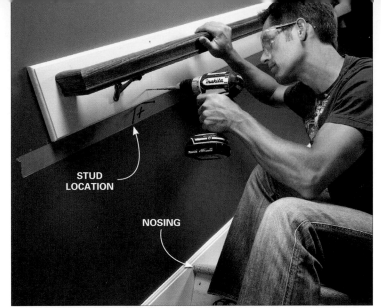

STUD
LOCATION

NOSING

Start by measuring the distance from the nosing at the top landing to the nosing on the bottom tread. Add 12 in. to this measurement to find the length of the board you'll need. We used a 1x6 and shaped the edge with a router and cove bit. Cut the handrail 6 in. longer than your measurement with 45-degree miters on each end. Screw the handrail brackets to the handrail (but not the board yet), spacing them about 4 ft. apart and about 1 ft. from each end. Support the handrail on the board and measure from the tip of the miter to the board to find the length of the returns. Cut the returns. Then glue and nail them to the ends on the handrail. Photos 1–3 show how to complete the job. We used finish screws to attach the board to the wall because the heads are smaller and easier to hide.

2. Screw the board to the studs. Position a strip of masking tape parallel to the stairs with the top edge located so that the top of the rail will be 34 to 36 in. above the stair nosings. Locate the studs and mark them on the tape. Support the handrail board on a pair of nails. Drive a pair of 3-in. screws into every other stud.

TEMPORARY
SUPPORT

3. Screw the brackets to the board. Complete the job by straightening the brackets and screwing them to the board. Use the screws provided with the handrail brackets.

Replace a bad deck board

As decks age, the deck boards (the ones you walk on) take a real beating. Sometimes so many of the boards are bad that you should replace all of them. If the structure below them is in good shape, a great project is to replace all the wood decking with new no-maintenance plastic or wood-plastic composite decking. But sometimes there are just a couple boards that are bad, either from splitting or rot. Then it's time to simply replace the bad ones. It's an easy process, as these photos show. Here are a few additional tips:

➤ Replace your bad deck boards with ones of the same species, either redwood, cedar or treated pine. Don't worry about the color difference; you can finish them for a better match later.

➤ Buy galvanized nails or screws (depending on what's already there) that will go through the decking and penetrate the joists below by at least 1-1/2 in.

➤ Position the new deck boards so the growth rings you see on the cut ends are concave-down. They'll be less likely to cup and split as they weather.

1. Cut out the bad section with a jigsaw. Use a square to guide the saw, and cut directly alongside a joist at each end of the cut.

JIGSAW

SPEED SQUARE

2. Nail a cleat to the joist to support the end of the new board. The cleat should be 12 in. long and pulled tightly underneath the deck boards on either side.

CLEAT

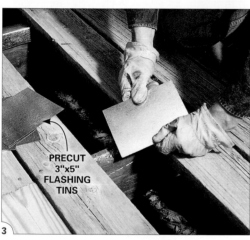

PRECUT 3"x5" FLASHING TINS

3. If the top edge of a joist is slightly soft or rotted, brush on some wood preservative, place a piece of metal flashing on the joist and bend down the edges.

FLATTEN NAIL TIP

4. Nail or screw on the new deck board, being very careful not to split the ends. If you're nailing, flatten the tip of the nail before driving it. Drill pilot holes for screws.

Chapter **6**

Backyard Improvements

Plant a potted tree

With the proper planting and watering techniques, you can give your new tree the best chance of surviving the first critical years, and prevent problems that could limit the tree's growth in the future.

Here you'll discover a simple method for planting a potted tree using the latest information gleaned from leading national tree experts.

Shown here is a relatively large container-grown Autumn Blaze maple tree. It is much lighter and easier to handle than a comparably sized balled and burlapped (B&B) tree. If you decide to purchase a B&B tree instead, see "Planting a Balled & Burlapped Tree," p. 150, for special instructions. Bare-root trees are available in the spring and offer a great value if you're willing to wait a few extra years for a good-size tree. For bare-root trees, dig a hole wide enough to spread the roots

and just deep enough to set the trunk flare slightly above the soil level. Then follow the same planting, staking and watering instructions shown here.

Spring and fall are the best times to plant most trees. If you decide to plant a tree in the summer, make sure you water it frequently enough.

Determine your soil type

Most trees grow best in well-drained soil. It's a good idea to perform a simple test in the location you'll be planting the tree to see how well the soil drains. Photo 1 shows how. If you still have standing water in the hole after 24 hours, shop for a species that can tolerate wet conditions. In addition, plant the tree shallower to avoid suffocating the roots. (See "Planting a Tree in Clay Soil," p. 147). For well-drained soil, follow our planting method.

1. Test the soil drainage by digging a hole 24 in. deep at the future tree location and fill it with water. Let the water completely drain into the soil and then fill the hole again. Wait 24 hours and check it. If it's empty, you have well-drained soil and a good planting site. A hole half full of water indicates very poor drainage. Choose a new site or use special planting techniques (p. 147).

Transport your tree carefully

Potted trees usually come in a 10-gallon container (3/4-in. to 1-in.-diameter trunk) or a 25-gallon container (1-1/2-in. to 1-3/4-in.-diameter trunk). Twenty-five gallon container trees weigh about 150 lbs., which is about the most you can get home yourself. If you decide to transport the tree yourself, wrap the tree trunk in a blanket to protect it from scrapes and damaged bark. If you choose a heavy B&B tree, ask the nursery if it can be delivered and placed near your planting spot.

Find the trunk flare

Planting your tree too deep can suffocate the roots and contribute to a condition called "stem girdling roots," in which roots wrap around the base of the trunk and choke off the supply of water and nutrients. The top of the trunk flare (Photo 2) should be slightly above the level of the soil when you're

2. Dig into the soil to find the spot where the large roots flare out from the trunk (the trunk flare). Measure down from the top of the pot to the top of the trunk flare and record the measurement.

3. Measure the height of the pot and subtract the distance down to the trunk flare. Dig your planting hole about 1 in. shallower than this calculated dimension.

through planting. You can see in Photo 2 that we had to dig down about 5 in. to find the trunk flare. Photos 2–5 show how to determine the depth of the planting hole.

Prepare the planting bed

To reduce competition for nutrients and water, remove the sod in a circle around the tree (Photo 4). Loosening the soil makes it easier for new roots to penetrate the soil and for water to soak in.

Dig the hole just deep enough to support the root ball and leave the top of the root flare above ground level (Photo 8). In good, loose soil, there's no need to dig the hole any wider than about 1-1/2 times the diameter of the container. If the soil is hard to dig and seems compacted, enlarge the planting hole to about three times the diameter of the pot but keep the depth the same. The extra volume of loosened soil will make it easier for the new roots to get established.

4. Skim off the sod in a circle at least 5 ft. in diameter with a sharp spade. Then loosen the soil to about 8 in. deep with a garden fork.

5. Dig the planting hole to the calculated depth and about 1-1/2 times the diameter of the pot.

Planting a tree in clay soil

If the drainage test (Photo 1) shows that your soil drains poorly, follow the planting details shown here. Digging a standard-depth hole in clay soil will only make the problem worse. The goal is to prevent the roots from suffocating in a hole filled with soggy clay soil. Dig the planting hole so that only half of the root ball is below the surrounding soil. Then refill the planting hole with a 50/50 mix of good black dirt and the clay soil you removed. Haul in enough good soil to pile up to the root ball and slope down to grade to form a 6- to 10-ft.-diameter circle. Cover the new soil with a 2-in. layer of organic mulch such as wood chips or bark.

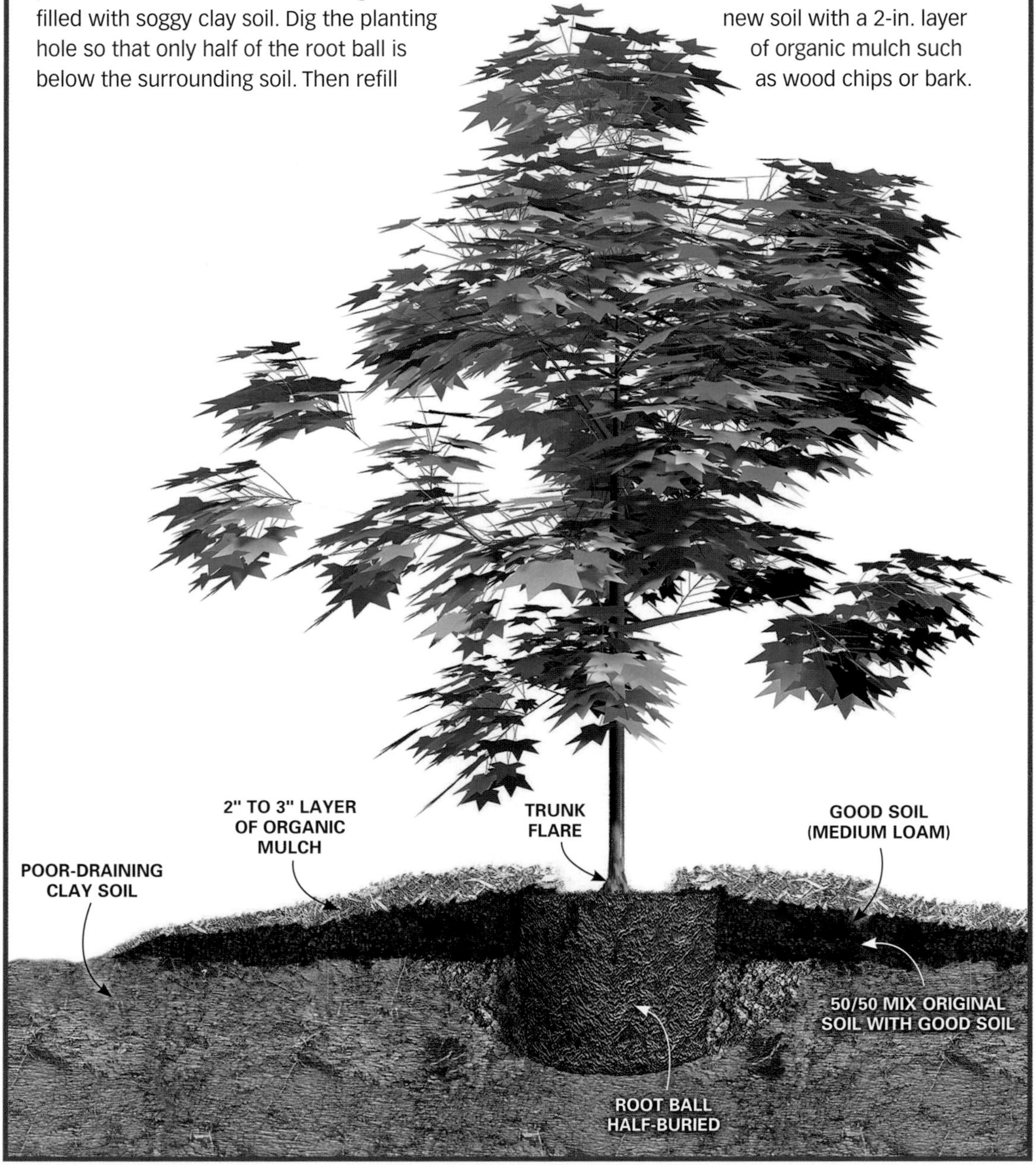

POOR-DRAINING CLAY SOIL

2" TO 3" LAYER OF ORGANIC MULCH

TRUNK FLARE

GOOD SOIL (MEDIUM LOAM)

50/50 MIX ORIGINAL SOIL WITH GOOD SOIL

ROOT BALL HALF-BURIED

SLICE OFF
BOTTOM

6. Cut the plastic bottom from the pot with a sharp utility knife. Carefully slide the tree into the hole and stand it up. Stand back and look at the tree from two directions to make sure it's standing straight.

Cut encircling roots

It's not uncommon for the roots of container-grown trees to begin circling around the inside of the pot. To prevent encircling roots from strangling the plant later, and to encourage them to grow out into the surrounding soil, slice them with a utility knife as shown in Photo 7 or tear the roots loose with your fingers and spread them in the planting hole. New roots will grow from the cut ends, helping to anchor the tree. Follow the instructions in Photo 8 to refill the hole with dirt.

Prevent weeds and conserve moisture with mulch

A 3- to 4-in.-deep layer of wood chips or other organic mulch helps hold in moisture and keeps weeds and grass from taking root. It also serves as a buffer zone to protect the tree trunk from lawn mower and string trimmer damage. Keep the mulch about 6 in. away from the trunk to allow air to circulate around the trunk and prevent

SNIP
THICK
RIM

SLICE
SIDE

SLICE
ENCIRCLING
ROOTS

7. Slice the side of the container and cut the thicker rim with a pruner or tin snips. Remove the pot from the root ball. Make four vertical slices through encircling roots with a utility knife.

bark diseases. If you live in an area where rodents burrow under snow and chew on bark, protect the trunk with a wire mesh screen (Photo 9).

There's no hard and fast rule about staking

Most experts agree that a tree will develop a stronger trunk if it's allowed to sway in the breeze. On the other hand, too much movement can tear new roots and prevent the tree from getting established. And in windy areas, trees with lightweight rootballs can blow over. If you plant the tree in an area that's exposed to wind, stake it for the first year. Potted trees are more likely to need staking because their root balls are not as heavy as those of balled and

SLICE SOIL
TO SETTLE

8. Refill the planting hole about halfway with the soil you removed. Eyeball the tree as you fill the hole to make sure it's still standing straight up. Slice down around the root ball about 20 or 30 times with a spade to break up clumps and settle the soil. Pour about 20 gallons of water around the plant to settle the soil and moisten the roots. When the water drains, fill the remainder of the hole with soil, slice it down with the shovel, and water it again to settle the soil.

Planting a balled & burlapped tree

If you choose a B&B tree rather than a potted tree like ours, you'll only have to modify the planting process slightly. First, establish the proper planting depth by probing around the trunk with a stiff wire like a clothes hanger to find the trunk flare (Photo 2). Otherwise you'd have to untie the wrapping and risk disturbing the root ball before you lower the plant into the hole.

Cut the wire loop from the bottom of the ball with a heavy-duty wire cutter or bolt cutter. Gently roll the ball into the hole, stand it up, and remove the remainder of the wire basket. Then slice off the burlap or synthetic material just as if it were a plastic pot. Removing all the wrapping material like this will prevent it from interfering with the root growth later.

Eyeball the tree to make sure it's standing straight. Then fill around the root ball (Photo 8) and complete the job by mulching and staking if necessary (Photo 10).

burlapped trees. It's better to err on the side of caution, since it only takes about half an hour to drive stakes and add ties.

Photo 10 shows a method of staking that's strong and durable. You'll find the metal "T" posts at most home centers and some lumberyards. Bike inner tubes make perfect tree ties because they stretch, allowing some movement, and they're wide and soft, so they won't damage the bark. Check at your local bike store for old tubes or buy new ones. Loop the ties about one-third to halfway up the trunk.

Water frequently with less water

Many trees grow slowly or die because they're not watered frequently enough. The old recommendation of an inch of water a week is not sufficient for most trees. Here's what the experts recommend. Multiply the diameter of the trunk by 2 to arrive at the number of gallons of water to use. Then water every day with this amount for the first two weeks. A tree with a 2-in. diameter trunk, for example, would require 4 gallons of water every day for two weeks. Then water every two or three days for the next two months. After that, water once or

9. Protect the bark of your new tree from rodents by surrounding it with a hardware cloth cage. Cut a 20 x 20-in. square of 1/4-in. mesh hardware cloth with tin snips. Form a 6-in. diameter tube around the tree with the hardware cloth and secure it with a wrap of 14-gauge wire. Bend clothes hangers into 6-in. long J-shaped stakes and push them into the ground around the tube to hold it down.

twice a week for 12 to 18 months. As the tree gets bigger, increase the amount of water accordingly. Pour the water slowly over the root ball. Use less water and water less often if you have poorly drained soil.

Too much water is harmful too. The low-tech method for testing soil moisture is to simply stick your finger into the soil of the root ball. Do this every time before you water. If the soil is saturated, don't water.

Wait to prune and fertilize

Fertilizing your new tree isn't necessary and may even be harmful. It may be beneficial to fertilize your tree after the second year. Ask your grower to recommend a fertilizing schedule for your tree. Trim off broken or dead branches but don't prune to shape until the second year.

10. Drive two 7-ft. metal fence posts about 1 ft. from the trunk and on opposite sides of the tree. Cut a bike inner tube in half, loop it around the tree and knot the ends together to form a loop. Twist 14-gauge wire around each knot and around the metal posts. Leave a little slack in the inner tube to allow the tree to move. Remove the stakes after one year.

PROFESSIONAL
COST: $150

YOUR COST: $0

SAVINGS: $150

COMPLEXITY
Easy

TOOLS
Pruning shears
Pruning saw
Bow saw
Lopping shears
Pole saw

MATERIALS
None

Trim a tree

Trees are an important part of any yard. And as any tree owner knows, they need occasional trimming. Properly done, trimming controls the shape of the tree, keeps the tree healthy, and eliminates branches that endanger property or could potentially interfere with overhead wires or nearby structures.

Rather than using the haphazard hacking approach, with the right equipment and a little patience, you can trim your own trees and save a bundle over hiring a professional tree trimmer. A word of advice: The most common mistake is to over-trim a long-neglected tree. If you haven't had the pruning saw out for a long time, take it easy!

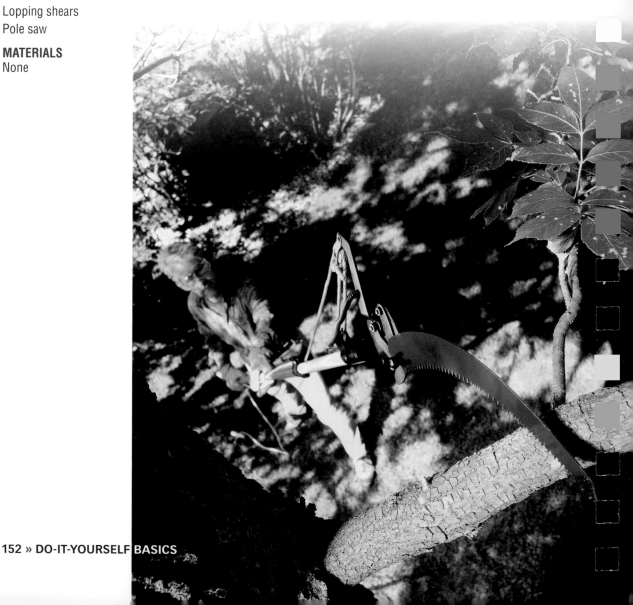

The anatomy of a tree

In trimming, the most important parts of the tree are the buds (Figure A and inset). The direction the tree will grow is determined by the buds. When trimming, spare the buds that are pointed in the direction you want the tree to grow.

The terminal (end) buds continue the outward or upward growth of the branch. The removal of a terminal bud causes the growth of side branches, making the tree bushier.

Figure A
Tree terminology

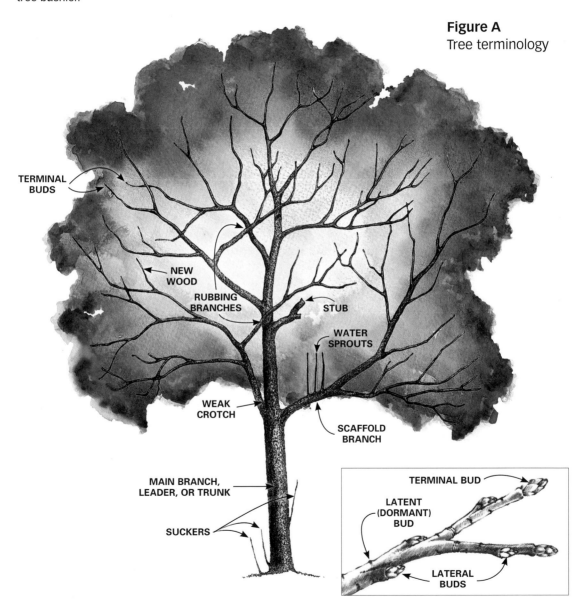

TERMINAL BUDS

NEW WOOD

RUBBING BRANCHES

STUB

WATER SPROUTS

WEAK CROTCH

SCAFFOLD BRANCH

MAIN BRANCH, LEADER, OR TRUNK

SUCKERS

TERMINAL BUD

LATENT (DORMANT) BUD

LATERAL BUDS

Buds that lie dormant for many years are called latent buds. They may only start to grow after the tree has sustained damage to other branches.

Proper trimming technique

The photo below shows the best way to trim a branch larger than 2 in. The initial undercut is important, as it prevents the weight of a trimmed branch from pulling a big strip of bark off the tree. Your goal, as shown in Figure B, is a cut that's close to the trunk, angled up and flush with the branch collar.

When to cut

The best time to trim living branches (dead branches can be trimmed any time) is late winter, when the tree is dormant, or very early in the spring prior to new growth. Technically, most trees can be trimmed any time, but some trees are more susceptible to disease and infestation if trimmed in the summer. Elms and oaks should be trimmed in the dormant season to reduce the chance of developing Dutch elm disease or oak wilt.

What to cut

When you're ready to trim, you'll have to decide what to cut and what to leave alone. You should look for:

> **Dead or dying branches.** Cut them back to another healthy branch or back to the main trunk. If trimming a diseased tree, be sure to disinfect tools between each cut.

> **Branch stubs.** Remove all too-long stubs back to the nearest healthy branch or trunk.

> **Chances to correct the tree's shape.** Familiarize yourself with how the tree should look naturally. An ideal tree has a strong central trunk and scaffold limbs that are spaced along the trunk with no two of them directly above and shading the other branches.

> **Branches growing too close together.** The process of removing excess branches is called thinning. It opens up the tree to let in air and light for the leaves on the inside and lower portions of the tree, improving fruit and flower production.

> **Rubbing branches.** Remove any branches that rub against each other or might in the future. These branches often develop open wounds where insects can enter and disease can start.

> **Suckers and water sprouts (see Figure A).** Remove suckers growing at the base and trunk of the tree and water sprouts growing vertical to the trunk.

> **Weak crotches.** Remove branches that have weak or narrow-angle (less than 30 degrees) crotches. These branches are the most likely to tear away in storms, damaging the bark and nearby branches.

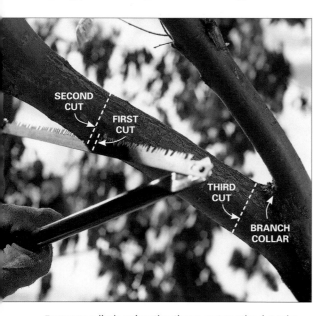

Remove a limb using the three-cut method. Make the first cut (an undercut) from below, about 12 in. from the trunk and approximately one-third of the limb's thickness. Make the second cut from above, about 1 in. out from the undercut, going completely through the limb. The third cut removes the small remaining piece of limb.

What about safety?

First off, always wear eye protection and gloves when trimming trees. Second, stay away from all utility wires.

If you must remove a large limb over a patio or close to your house or garage, take steps to reduce the risk of damage as it drops. One good way to control the drop is to tie a rope around the limb to be cut and throw the other end of the rope over a higher limb. Have a helper keep just enough tension on the rope to control the limb without binding the saw blade. **Caution:** Watch for the thick end of the limb as it falls. If the job just seems too dangerous to tackle yourself, don't hesitate to call a certified arborist.

Figure B Cutting technique

RIGHT
MINIMAL STUMP, NO BARK DAMAGE, ANGLE MINIMIZES WOUND SIZE

WRONG
TOO CLOSE TO BARK RIDGE

BARK RIDGES

WRONG
TOO MUCH STUMP

Correct cutting technique prevents damage to the bark and bark ridges, leaving a clean, slightly angled cut that produces the smallest wound, and avoids long stumps, which are avenues for insect infestation and rot. Always use sharp tools for the cleanest cuts.

The right tools make all the difference

If you buy a few moderately priced tools and rent others as needed, you'll be able to properly maintain your trees for years. With good pruning shears, you'll be able to cut flush with the branch collar. Position the thin blade on the trunk side to keep the resulting stub as short as you want it to be. Use the shears for branches up to 1/2 in. thick.

If you have to struggle with the shears, you should move up to the lopping shears. You'll be able to cut branches around 1-in. thick with loppers. For larger branches, use a pruning saw or a bow saw. Never use a regular shop saw because it will require much more effort and it won't do a good job.

For really high branches, you can rent or buy a pole saw. Some have a small curved saw on the end and others have a cord- or rod-operated lever-action pruning shear.

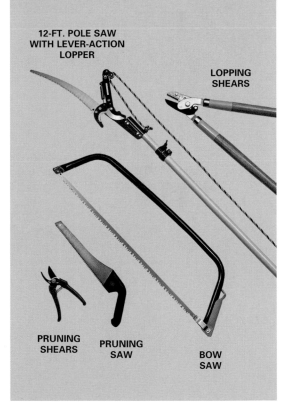

12-FT. POLE SAW WITH LEVER-ACTION LOPPER

LOPPING SHEARS

PRUNING SHEARS

PRUNING SAW

BOW SAW

PROFESSIONAL
COST: $1,000

YOUR COST: $500

SAVINGS: $500

COMPLEXITY
Simple

TOOLS
Rake
Level
Safety glasses
Sledgehammer
Spade
Tape measure
Wheelbarrow
Sod cutter

MATERIALS
Sand
Flagstone
Retaining wall stones
Spray paint

Build a stone fire ring

An outdoor fire is a natural gathering spot for family and friends, whether for a cookout or casual conversation on a cool evening.

You can make those gatherings more comfortable and safe by building a simple fire ring with retaining wall stone. To complete the setting, we'll show you how to surround the ring with flagstone. It more comfortably accommodates chairs and benches and eliminates the inevitable mud pit that comes with wet weather.

This project requires no special tools or skills. In fact, the primary tool for this project is a strong back! You'll be lifting and moving heavy stone, both for the fire ring and for the surround. Rent or borrow a two-wheel dolly to ease the load if you have to move the stone far. A manual sod cutter (Photo 2) simplifies the digging, but it also takes some strength to operate. A good shovel is easier to use but quite a bit slower.

For this project we ordered:

➤ 24 granite retaining wall stones (6-1/2 x 8 x 14 in.)

➤ 200 sq. ft. of flagstone (Chilton)

➤ 1-1/2 yds. of sand

Once you have the materials on site, you can complete this project in one (long!) day.

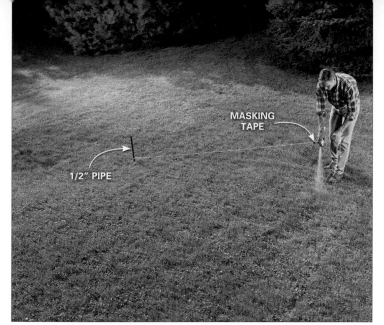

1. Drive a pipe firmly into the ground at the center of the fire ring. Loop a string over the stake and measure out 9 ft. Mark this point with tape. Hold a can of marking spray paint at the tape and spray the complete circle.

2. Cut away the sod with a sod cutter. Follow the perimeter and then cut away the inside of the circle. Leave the pipe in place.

Site planning and ring assembly

Begin your planning with a call to your local building department to learn about local fire restrictions. Many regions require burning permits and restrict the size of a fire ring.

Choose an area that's about 18 ft. in diameter and relatively flat. Be sure to locate the fire ring away from trees, bushes and buildings. Remember that burning wood snaps and pops, sending sparks into the air.

Drive a pipe at the center and mark out a 9-ft. radius circle (Photo 1). Remove the sod or plant material and enough dirt so the paving stones you've chosen are flush with the surrounding grass when set in 1 in. of sand (Photos 2 and 3). The sod cutter we show operates with a firm stomp on the crossbar. It takes a little practice and strength to cut the sod smoothly. Wear heavy boots and gloves when using it.

While you want your fire ring to sit level, the surrounding flagstone sitting area can follow the contours of the yard, its edges blending with the sod (Photo 3). However, if you have from 1 to 3 ft. of rise over the 18-ft. diameter of the sitting area, consider excavating the high side to keep the sitting area reasonably level. Then build a small retaining wall to hold back the soil. This actually makes for a nice design. The retaining wall becomes a sitting area as well as a shelf and serving counter.

We chose granite retaining wall stones for the ring. They're a uniform size and easy to fit together tightly, and their weight (about 70 lbs.) makes them stable. Other types of retaining wall stone, including concrete, will work too.

3. Remove enough dirt so that the top of the flagstone sits 1 in. below the surrounding sod. The sod cutter works well for shaving down the grade, but a flat shovel works well too.

4. Drive a 6-in. landscape spike beside the center pipe until it's 2 in. below the sod level. Drive six additional spikes about 3 ft. away from the center, spacing them evenly around the center. Level the top of each spike with the center one, then spread sand in the circle flush with the tops of the spikes.

70-LB. BLOCKS

21" RADIUS

5. Draw a 21-in. radius circle with the string and marking paint. Lay the first row of retaining wall stones (12 in our case) along the line, minimizing the gaps between them. Twist each stone back and forth a few times in the sand to firmly set it. Make the tops level.

Lay the stones in a circle to determine how large to make the ring. There's no exact rule here. A 42-in. inner diameter works well, but you can adjust the size according to preference and code. Measure the radius of the circle and then mark this circle at the center of your fire ring (Photo 5).

To avoid pinched toes or fingers, limit the height of the ring to about 12 in., or two rows of stone. If you go higher, keep in mind that the stones can slip off and fall, especially if you use smaller, less stable stones.

It's important to set the stones on a level bed of sand to keep the base stones stable and the joints tight. Stretch a string tightly across the circle to establish the height of the sod, and follow Photo 4 to create the sand bed.

Use a carpenter's level to accurately align the tops of the first row of stones (Photo 4). Minimize the gaps between stones. The second row goes up fast—you simply set it on top of the first.

6. Set the second row of stones on top of the first. Straddle the joints of the first row.

Lay the sitting area

Many types of materials will make a nice sitting area: various gravels; stone, brick or concrete pavers; flagstones; or even poured concrete. Irregular flagstones with grass planted between them gave us an attractive, informal look. A flagstone sitting area is easy to lay and easy to maintain. Just run the lawn mower over the stones to trim the grass.

Set the flagstones in a bed of sand, letting them follow the contour of the ground (Photos 7 and 8). To minimize tripping, make a special effort to keep the edges flush.

TWIST STONE INTO PLACE

RAKED SAND

7. Spread 1 in. of sand over the sitting area. Fit the first flagstone tightly to the fire ring. Twist it into the sand to firmly set it. If it rocks, add or remove sand to stabilize it.

SLEDGE-HAMMER

BREAK LARGER STONES AS NEEDED

8. Fit and set stones out to the circle's edge. Keep the flagstone edges flush to one another and leave 2- to 4-in. spaces in between. You can break larger flagstones with a sledgehammer. **Caution:** Wear eye protection when breaking stone.

KITCHEN
KNIFE

TOPSOIL

Because we wanted a finished look right away, we meticulously cut and fitted sod between the stones. In truth, it's a whole lot easier to completely fill the gaps with topsoil and sow grass seed. Or, instead of grass, you might consider ground covers suitable for your climate.

Finally, add about 4 in. of sand or gravel to the inside of the fire ring to raise the level of the fire. This will make it easier to tend. Then build a fire on the next cool evening and see how many neighbors it attracts.

9. Fill the spaces between the stones with topsoil to about 1/2 in. below the top. Then cut sod with a knife to fit between the stones. Press the sod firmly into the soil and keep the sod damp until it has rooted.

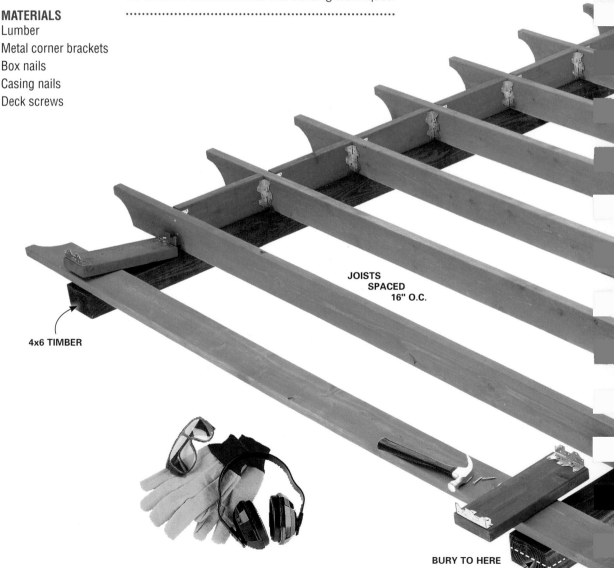

Build a simple deck

PROFESSIONAL COST: $1,100

YOUR COST: $500

SAVINGS: $600

COMPLEXITY
Moderate

TOOLS
See list on p. 163

MATERIALS
Lumber
Metal corner brackets
Box nails
Casing nails
Deck screws

You may not have a beachfront view, but you'll enjoy relaxing on this simple deck wherever you choose to build it. Since it's at ground level and is freestanding, you don't have to fuss with challenging railings or footings. All you need are basic carpentry tools and a relatively flat area in your yard or garden. The foundation is nothing more than 4x6 treated timbers buried in the soil, with decorative treated joists and construction-grade cedar decking and a bench. Follow the instructions along with the photos for detailed measurements and building techniques.

JOISTS SPACED 16" O.C.

4x6 TIMBER

BURY TO HERE

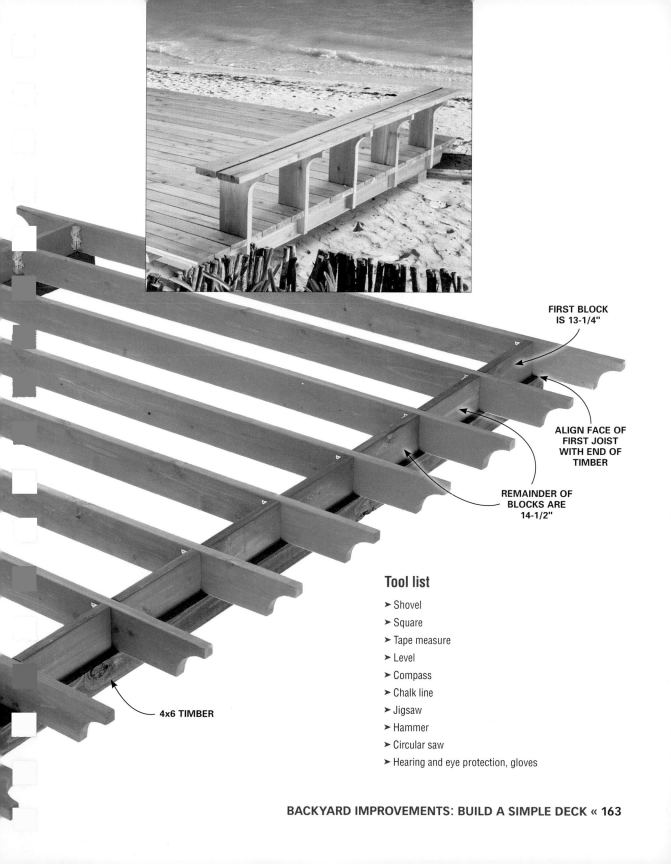

**FIRST BLOCK
IS 13-1/4"**

**ALIGN FACE OF
FIRST JOIST
WITH END OF
TIMBER**

**REMAINDER OF
BLOCKS ARE
14-1/2"**

4x6 TIMBER

Tool list

- ➤ Shovel
- ➤ Square
- ➤ Tape measure
- ➤ Level
- ➤ Compass
- ➤ Chalk line
- ➤ Jigsaw
- ➤ Hammer
- ➤ Circular saw
- ➤ Hearing and eye protection, gloves

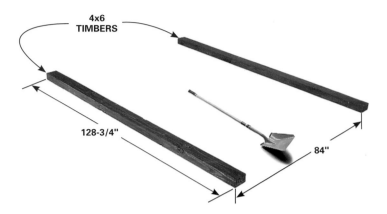

1. Dig the 4x6 timbers into the soil, leaving about 1-1/2 in. of the top exposed. The timbers must be parallel and the diagonal measurements must be equal.

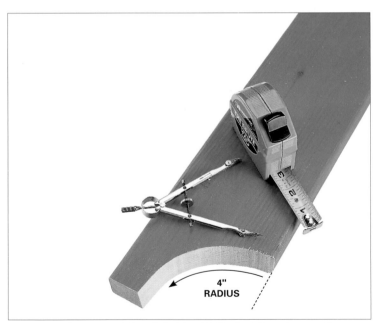

2. Cut each treated 2x6 joist to 10 ft. Cut the decorative curve on each end as shown before installing them onto the 4x6 treated timbers.

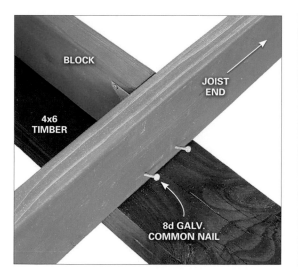

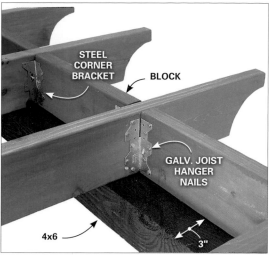

3. Lay out the joist spacing so the joists are on 16-in. centers. Cut the blocks to fit between the joists. The first set of blocks (one on each side) will be 13-1/4 in., while the remainder will be 14-1/2 in. long. Toenail each joist to the timber as shown. Be sure the ends of all the joists align with each other as you toenail them in place.

4. Nail your steel corner brackets to the joists and each block between with 1-1/4 in. galvanized joist hanger nails. The blocks add stability and give the deck a finished look.

pro tips!

➤ Toenailing is driving a nail at an angle through the end of a board to anchor it. It makes a strong joint and is a great way to coax stubborn boards into position.

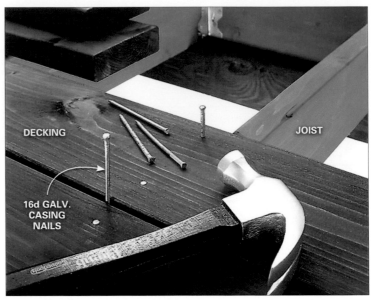

5. Start nailing the 2x6 decking from one side, leaving a 1-1/2 in. overhang. Keep the decking straight and use a 16d galvanized nail as a spacer. Depending on the spacing, you may need to rip the last piece of decking to maintain the 1-1/2 in. overhang.

6. Once the decking is nailed, crosscut the lengths, leaving a 1-1/2 in. overhang. Be sure to use a chalk line to establish a straight guideline before cutting.

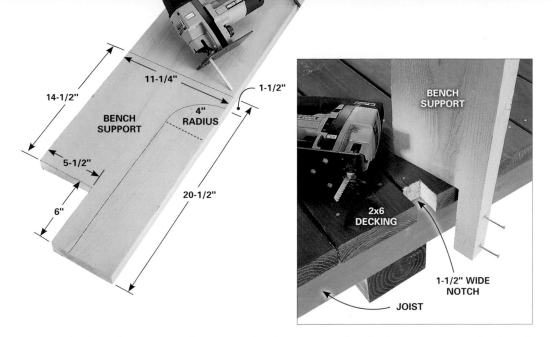

7. Cut the bench supports from 2x12 lumber. Notch the decking to accept the bench supports. Be sure to toenail the back side of the seat support to the decking for added stability. Be sure the supports are square to the deck surface, then screw the 2x6 bench tops to the supports with 3-in. galvanized screws.

Materials list

2	4x6 x 12' treated timbers
9	2x6 x 10' cedar joists
2	2x6 x 10' cedar for blocking
1	2x12 x 10' cedar bench supports
2	2x6 x 10' cedar bench tops
22	2x6 x 12' cedar decking
32	metal corner brackets
3 lbs.	galv. joist hanger nails
2 lbs.	No. 8 galv. box nails
10 lbs.	16d galv. casing nails
1 lb.	3" galv. deck screws

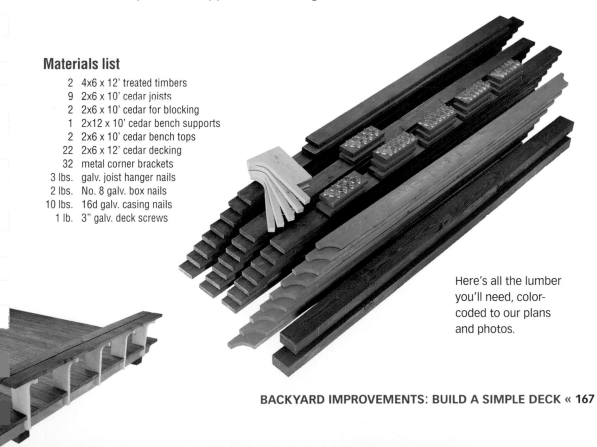

Here's all the lumber you'll need, color-coded to our plans and photos.

Install a stepping-stone path

Stepping-stone paths offer many of the advantages of concrete sidewalks and paver stone but without all the work, expense and mess. You can save wear and tear on your lawn in heavily used routes or take a trip to the garden without getting your feet wet from the morning dew. Since you only remove enough sod to place the stones, you can lay this path without tearing up your lawn. And if you pile the dirt and sod on a tarp as you work, cleanup can be easy too.

Almost any type of flat stones will work as long as they're about 2 in. thick. We picked these limestone stepping-stones from a pile at the local landscape supply center. You'll also need a 60-lb. bag of playground sand for every 10 stones.

1. Space the stepping-stones along the path to match your stride. Using the stones as patterns, cut through the sod around each stone with a drywall saw or a bread knife.

LIMESTONE STEPPING-STONES

DRYWALL KEYHOLE SAW

2. Move the stone to the side and dig out the sod with a trowel. Dig the hole 1 in. deeper than the thickness of the stone to allow for the sand base.

3. Roughly level a 1-in. layer of sand in the hole. Set the stone on the sand and wiggle it until it's flush with the surrounding sod. Add or remove sand as necessary.

1" LAYER OF SAND

Beginner Woodworking Projects

Cedar bath mat

We saw a cedar mat like this online for $35 and thought, "Hey, we can make a better one for less." The project is super simple, practical and versatile: It can be a bath mat, an entry mat for a patio or a drip-dry platform for wet shoes. Here are some planning and building tips:

➤ We chose cedar for its looks and rot-resistance. But any wood would be fine.

➤ This mat is 14-1/2 x 30 in., but you can make yours any size. Just be sure the slats are supported by runners no more than 15 in. apart.

➤ Large knots create weak spots, so you may need to buy extra lumber to get sections that are free of knots.

➤ Although the nail holes won't show, patch them with wood filler before sanding and finishing. Left exposed, the nail heads may rust and stain the floor.

➤ We finished this mat with tung oil. Oil finishes aren't as durable as some others, but they're easy to renew when the finish starts to wear—just wipe on a fresh coat.

➤ Be sure to apply anti-skid pads on the bottom to keep the mat from sliding on hard floors.

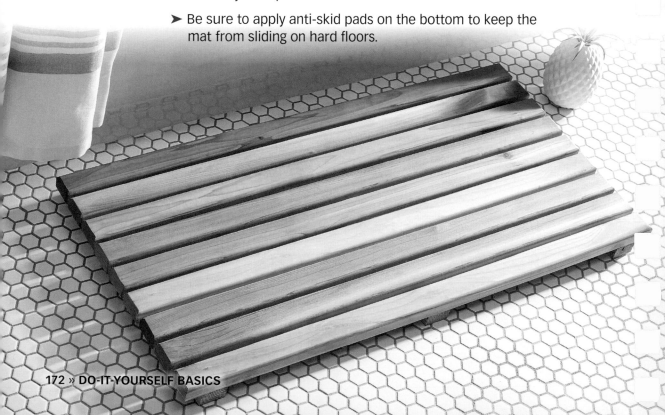

1. **Cut the slats.** If your local home center doesn't have good-quality 1x2 stock for the slats, buy a 1x6 and cut 1-1/2-in. strips. An 8-ft. 1x6 provided all the slats we needed.

2. **Round the edges.** We rounded the slat edges with a 1/4-in. round-over bit. If you don't have a router, ease the edges with 100-grit sandpaper.

SQUARE

RUNNER

SPACER

SLAT

3. **Assemble the mat.** Clamp wood scraps to your workbench to form a square. Lay out the slats against the guide using spacers cut from a paint stir stick. Then cut three runners 1 in. shorter than the width of the mat. Fasten the runners to the slats with 1-1/4-in. brads or nails.

Bagel holder

This bagel holder is as easy to build as it is to use. Making it requires only a few simple tools, two dowels and a scrap of hardwood. When you're hungry, drop the bagel in the cage, squeeze the dowel tops so the side dowels bend and pinch the bagel, then slice away. It keeps fingers out of harm's way (and the crumbs and knife blade off the counter).

Dowel diameters vary slightly. To ensure you get a good fit, drill a sample hole with your 3/16-in. brad point bit and take that scrap with you to test-fit the 3/16-in. dowels you buy.

Use mineral oil (available at drug stores) to finish your bagel holder. It's nontoxic dry or wet. (If you decide to use a different finish, be sure it's nontoxic when dry.)

Figure A
Bagel holder details

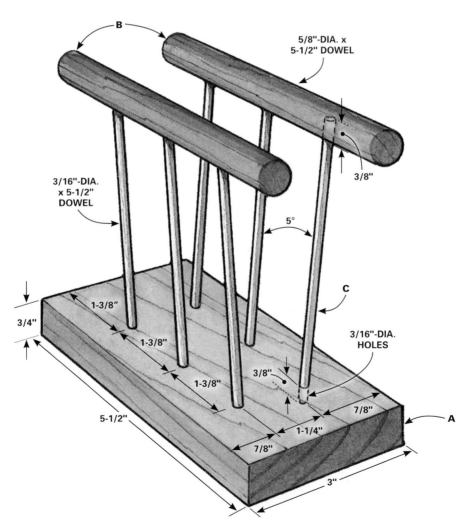

Build the bagel holder

Cut the dowels and hardwood base to the dimensions in the Cutting List on p. 177.

Lay out the holes in the base (Figure A). Make a drill guide by cutting a 5-degree angle on the end of a piece of scrap wood, then use it to guide your bit as you drill (Photo 1). Use a 2-in.-high guide and let the bit protrude 2-3/8 in. beyond the chuck. With this setup, when the chuck meets the top of the guide you'll get uniform 3/8-in.-deep holes.

Lay out the holes in the handles. Hold each in a vise or clamp while drilling the holes. Wrap a piece of masking tape 3/8 in. from the tip of your bit to act as a depth guide.

Glue and tap the uprights into the handles. Be careful not to damage the ends of the uprights that fit into the base. Then glue and tap the uprights into the base (Photo 2).

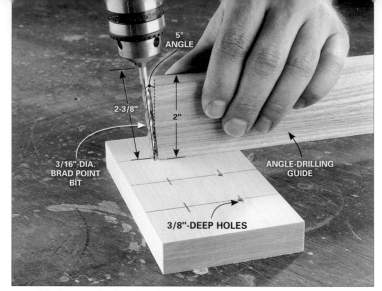

1. Drill the angled holes in the base. Guide the bit against the end of a 2-in.-wide piece of scrap wood with a 5-degree angle cut on the end. Set the bit in the chuck at a depth so that when the chuck hits the guide block, the hole is 3/8 in. deep.

2. Tap the preassembled dowel sides into the base using a rubber mallet. Start by inserting one of the end dowels, then work your way down to the other end. Glue all joints.

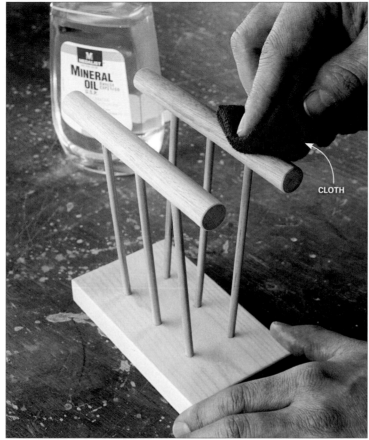

Let the glue dry, ease all the sharp edges with sandpaper, then apply a coat of mineral oil for the finish (Photo 3). Let the finish dry overnight.

CLOTH

3. Wipe on a coat of mineral oil to finish the wood.

Cutting List

KEY	QTY.	SIZE & DESCRIPTION
A	1	3/4" x 3" x 5-1/2" birch (base)
B	2	5/8"-dia. x 5-1/2" hardwood dowel (handles)
C	6	3/16"-dia. x 5-1/2" hardwood dowel (uprights)

Materials List

3/4" x 3" x 5-1/2" birch

5/8"-dia. x 12" hardwood dowel

3/16"-dia. x 36" hardwood dowel

Small bottle of mineral oil

Sturdy stool

This stool is as practical as it is beautiful. The crossed, flared legs make it stable, strong and quick to build.

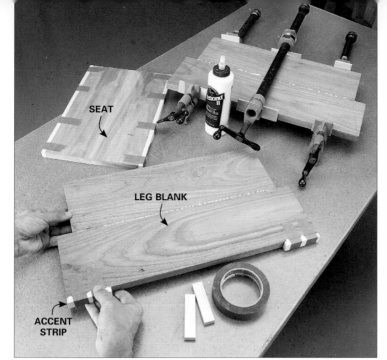

Start by gluing 4-1/2-in.-wide boards together (Photo 1) for the seat and 5-1/2-in.-wide boards for the legs. Rip 1/2-in.-wide contrasting accent strips on your table saw and glue them into place.

Next, mark the leg blanks, beginning with a center line (Photo 2). To mark the angled end cuts, measure 10 in. from the center line at the bottom and then draw a 15-degree angle. Make a trammel to mark the arcs: Drill a pencil hole in a strip of wood, then drive a screw 8 in. from the center of the pencil hole. Cut the arc with a jigsaw and sand it smooth. If your table saw is large enough, use it to cut the angled ends of the legs. Otherwise, use a circular saw and sand the cut smooth.

1. Glue and clamp boards together to form the top and legs. Add accent strips, using masking tape to hold the strips until the glue dries.

2. Mark the arcs with a homemade trammel. Draw center lines on the legs to accurately position the arcs, the end cuts and the notches you'll cut next.

Figure A
Sturdy stool

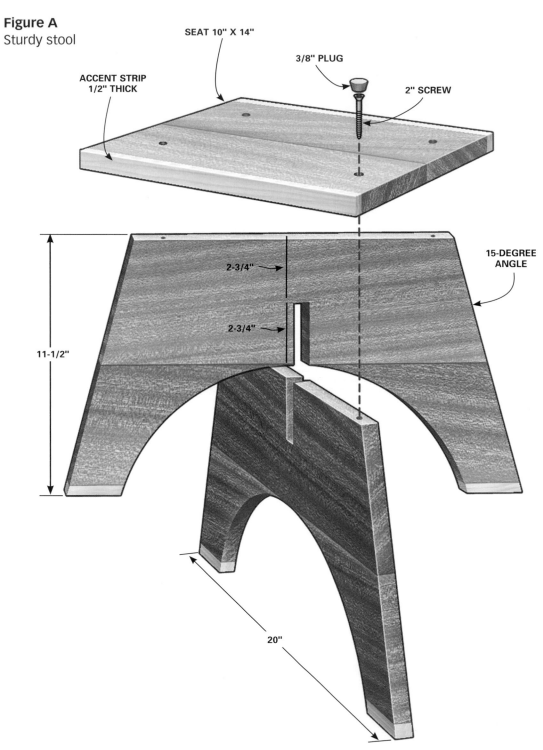

SEAT 10" X 14"

3/8" PLUG

2" SCREW

ACCENT STRIP
1/2" THICK

2-3/4"

2-3/4"

15-DEGREE
ANGLE

11-1/2"

20"

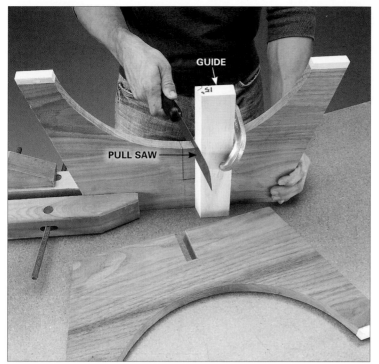

GUIDE

PULL SAW →

3. Cut perfect notches using a guide block to steer your saw. To make the guide, cut a scrap of wood on your table saw with the blade set to 15 degrees.

Materials List

- ➤ 10 ft. of walnut, 1x6
- ➤ 2 ft. of maple, 1x2
- ➤ Wood glue
- ➤ 2-in. screws
- ➤ 3/8-in. maple plugs
- ➤ Spray lacquer

pro tips!

➤ **Fast finishing.** Brushing a clear finish onto this project would be difficult. So we sprayed on two light coats of clear lacquer. Sand lightly with a fine-grit sanding sponge between coats. Lacquer dries very fast, so the whole process takes only about an hour.

Cut the notches in the legs with a small pull saw (Photo 3). With both sides of the notch cut, break out the middle and smooth the bottom of the notch with a chisel. Slip the two legs together. If light hammer taps won't drive the legs together, hone down the tight spots with a file.

With the seat lying upside down, set the leg assembly on it and trace the outline of the legs. Drill marker holes through the seat from the underside at each of the four screw locations using a 1/16-in. bit. Then flip the top over and drill a 3/8-in. hole 3/8 in. deep at each marker hole. Use a brad-point bit for these holes to avoid splintering. Set the seat on the legs, drill 1/8-in. pilot holes and screw the seat to the legs.

Swedish boot scraper

Here's a traditional Swedish farm accessory for gunk-laden soles. The dimensions are not critical, but be sure the edges of the slats are fairly sharp—they're what makes the boot scraper work. Cut slats to length, then cut triangular openings on the side of a pair of 2x2s. A radial arm saw works well for this, but a table saw or band saw will also make the cut. Trim the 2x2s to length, predrill and use galvanized screws to attach the slats from underneath.

SCREW FROM BELOW

2x2

SLAT

Sliding bookend

To corral shelf-dwelling books or DVDs that like to wander, cut 3/4-in.-thick hardwood pieces into 6-in. x 6-in. squares. Use a band saw or jigsaw to cut a slot along one edge (with the grain) that's a smidgen wider than the shelf thickness. Stop the notch 3/4 in. from the other edge. Finish the bookend and slide it on the shelf.

Chapter 8

Simple DIY Storage Solutions

How to install wire shelving

COMPLEXITY
Moderate

TOOLS
Bubble stick
Bolt cutter
Drill

MATERIALS
Standard wire
  shelving
Angle brackets, end
  brackets and clips
Extra parts
Pegboard (optional)

Wire shelving is popular because of its price, flexibility and ease of installation. Wire shelving can be designed to meet almost any need at a fraction of the cost of a custom built-in system. And while installing wire shelving isn't quite a no-brainer, you don't need to be a master carpenter or own a fully equipped cabinet shop to get it done. We picked the brain of a pro for these tips to help you on your next installation.

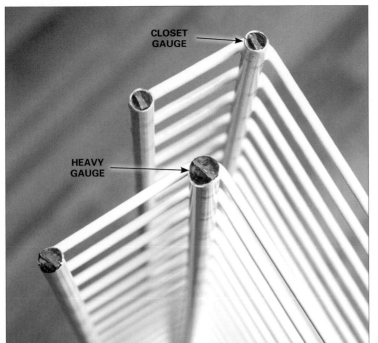

CLOSET GAUGE

HEAVY GAUGE

Leave the heavy stuff for the garage

Our pro primarily works with Closet Maid's standard wire shelving, sold at home centers. Most manufacturers make a heavier-duty product for garage storage, but he feels that the regular stuff is plenty strong for the average bedroom or hall closet. However, if your closet is going to store a bowling ball collection, you may want to consider upgrading. The materials for the closet shown here (approximately 22 ft. of shelving and rod) cost about $150.

....

BUBBLE STICK

Lay it out with a bubble stick

Our pro uses a bubble stick rather than a level. A bubble stick is like a ruler and a level rolled into one. Holding a level against the wall with one hand can be frustrating. Levels are rigid, and they pivot out of place when resting on a stud that's bowed out a bit. A bubble stick has a little flex, so it can ride the imperfections of the wall yet still deliver a straight line. You can get one at a hardware store or home center.

....

Use a template on the end brackets

Our pro's first template was nothing more than a 1x3 with a couple of holes drilled in it. He rested a torpedo level on top of the board and marked the end bracket locations with a pencil. The template he's using here has a built-in level and allows him to drill the holes without marking them first. At almost $200, this is for someone who installs lots of closet shelving. But if that's you, it's a great investment.

TEMPLATE

Buy extra pieces

Even if you're just planning to build one closet shelf, have extra parts on hand. It takes a lot less time to return a few wall clips than it does to stop working to make a special trip to the store for just one. And plans change, so if you decide to add a section of shelving, you'll be prepared.

A bolt cutter works best

Cut your shelving with a bolt cutter. It's quick and easy, and it makes a clean cut. To make room for the cutter, use your feet to hold the shelving off the ground.

ANGLE BRACKET

STUD

Space the angle brackets evenly

Consider aesthetics when installing the angle brackets. If a shelf only needs one bracket, find the stud closest to the center. If two or three brackets are required, try to space them evenly, making sure that at least one bracket toward the center is hitting a stud.

Measure an inch short

When cutting the shelf, measure wall to wall, and subtract an inch. This allows for the thickness of the end brackets plus a little wiggle room. It's the top, thinner wire that actually supports the shelf, and one wire per end is enough. Cutting exact lengths will only earn you wall scratches and a trip back to the cutting station.

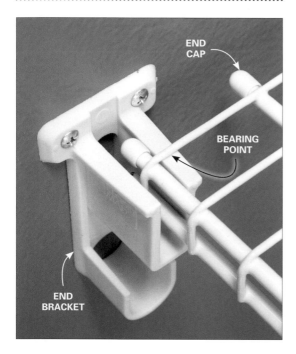

Pegboard prevents tipping

When our pro installs wire shelving in pantries, he likes to cap the top of shelves with white 1/4-in. pegboard. This stops the skinnier items from tipping over. He uses white zip ties to hold the pegboard in place. A 4 x 8-ft. sheet costs less than $20 at most home centers, which makes it an inexpensive option.

Avoid upheaval

Back wall clips are designed to support the shelf, but if there are a bunch of clothes hanging on the front of the shelf with nothing on top to weigh them down, the back of the shelf can lift. To keep the shelf in place, install a retaining clip in a stud near the middle of the shelf. One clip toward the middle of an 8-ft. shelf is plenty.

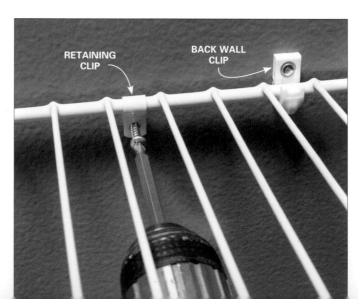

Back wall clips don't need to hit studs

It may go against your every instinct, but hitting a stud when you're installing the back wall clips slows the process down and isn't necessary. After marking their locations, drill a 1/4-in. hole and pop the preloaded pushpin in with a push tool. Our pro loves his push tool. It has a little indentation in the tip that won't slip off the pin when it's being set in the drywall. The occasional wall clips that do land on studs need to be fastened with a screw instead of a pin. You can order a push tool from your local Closet Maid dealer. It should cost less than $25. Use the dealer locator at closetmaid.com.

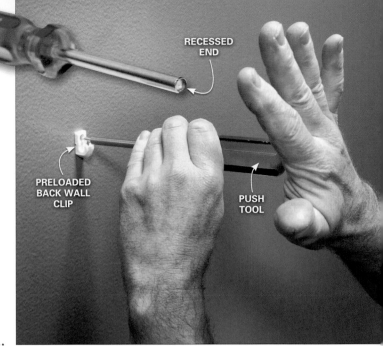

RECESSED END

PRELOADED BACK WALL CLIP

PUSH TOOL

CORNER HANGING BAR

BAR HANGER SUPPORT

Hanger sliding freedom

One common complaint about wire shelving is that it restricts the movement of the hangers because the hangers are stuck between the brackets. That's why our pro always offers the upgrade of a hanger rod. Most manufacturers make some version of one. A hanger rod allows clothes to be slid from one end of the closet to the other, even past an inside corner. This upgrade will add about 30 percent to the cost of the materials on a standard shelf design. Make sure the type of shelving you buy will work with the hanging rod hardware you plan to use.

**PROFESSIONAL
COST:** $200
per 4- x 8-ft. bay

YOUR COST: $80
per 4- x 8-ft. bay

**SAVINGS: $120
per 4- x 8-ft. bay**

COMPLEXITY
Moderate

TOOLS
Circular saw
Screw gun
Chalk line
4-ft. level

MATERIALS
Framing lumber
Pegboard
Wood glue
3-in. screws
1-1/2-in. washer-head
  screws
Adjustable shelf
  supports
Edge banding
Hinge supports

Complete garage storage system

The items on your garage walls may come and go as your hobbies and storage requirements evolve. The beauty of this system is that you can rearrange shelves, add or substitute pegboard accessories and even mount hanging systems that are designed for ordinary walls, so your wall will always suit your needs.

It's mostly framing lumber and pegboard

Check out Figure A to get the gist of the construction. After you establish the 2x2 grid work (see Figure B), you frame the perimeter with 2x10s. Then you cut the pegboard to fit and screw or glue it to the grid work. If you choose glue, you'll have to tack it in place until the glue sets. Then add the 2x8 partitions directly

over the pegboard seams. Use a 4-ft. level to make sure those are plumb so your shelves will fit in any location within each bay.

Screw all the framing in place by end-screwing or toe-screwing as needed with 3-in. screws. We show this project on a finished wall. But there's no reason you can't install it over exposed studs or even a concrete or block wall. If you're installing it over masonry, anchor the 2x2s with 3-in. concrete screw anchors (Tapcon is one brand). If the concrete is frequently damp, use treated 2x2s and they'll last forever.

Size it for your garage and storage needs

Think of this project in terms of 4- x 8-ft. bays. They can be vertical like ours or horizontal if that better fits your needs. Do one bay or as many as you want; the construction is the same.

Now, about the pegboard

If you're willing to shop around, you can find a lot of pegboard choices: thick, thin, metal, custom colors, etc. But if you shop at home centers or lumberyards, you generally only find 3/16-in.-thick plain brown and pegboard coated on one side with white melamine (Photo 5). Either one will work fine for this project. Get the plain stuff if you want to paint it a color or white if you're fine with that. If you do have choices, pick the thickest available with the larger (1/4-in.) holes.

While you're at the store, check out the pegboard accessories. You'll find all kinds of baskets, brackets, hooks, screwdriver holders, etc., designed to hang just about anything you can think of. Wait until the project is done and think it through before buying any, however.

Pegboard is dusty and messy to cut. Do it outside if you can or your entire garage and everything in it will be covered with dust. Wear a dust mask. Make your cuts with the good side down to eliminate tear-out on the show side.

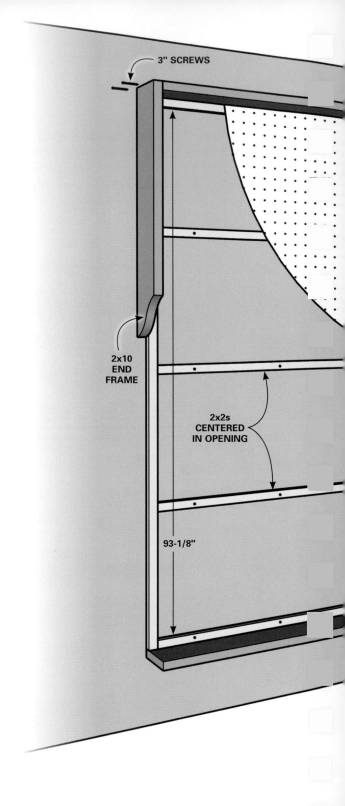

3" SCREWS

2x10 END FRAME

2x2s CENTERED IN OPENING

93-1/8"

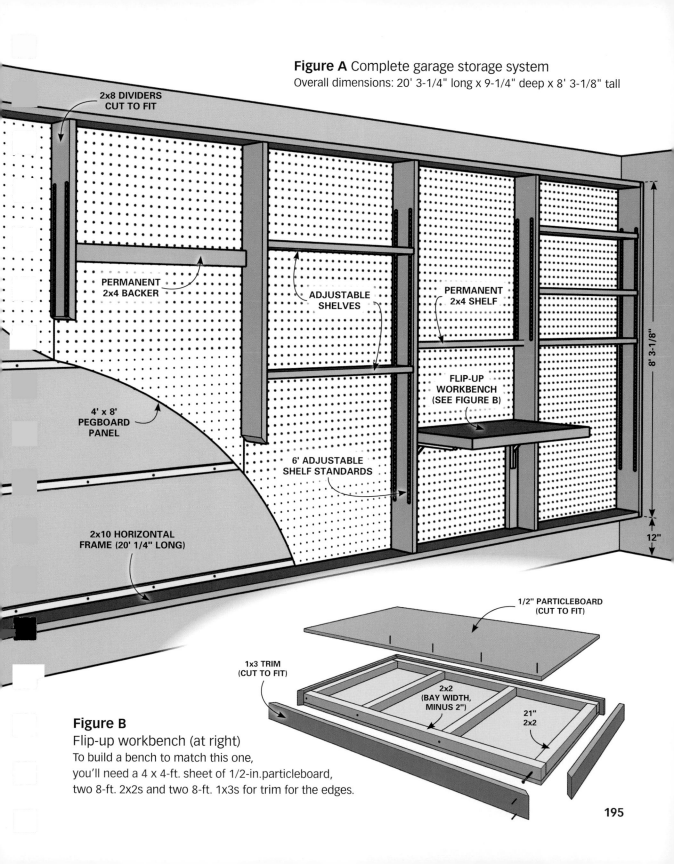

Figure A Complete garage storage system
Overall dimensions: 20' 3-1/4" long x 9-1/4" deep x 8' 3-1/8" tall

2x8 DIVIDERS
CUT TO FIT

PERMANENT
2x4 BACKER

ADJUSTABLE
SHELVES

PERMANENT
2x4 SHELF

4' x 8'
PEGBOARD
PANEL

FLIP-UP
WORKBENCH
(SEE FIGURE B)

6' ADJUSTABLE
SHELF STANDARDS

2x10 HORIZONTAL
FRAME (20' 1/4" LONG)

8' 3-1/8"

12"

1/2" PARTICLEBOARD
(CUT TO FIT)

1x3 TRIM
(CUT TO FIT)

2x2
(BAY WIDTH,
MINUS 2")

21"
2x2

Figure B
Flip-up workbench (at right)
To build a bench to match this one,
you'll need a 4 x 4-ft. sheet of 1/2-in.particleboard,
two 8-ft. 2x2s and two 8-ft. 1x3s for trim for the edges.

Write up a shopping list

It's impossible to give you a materials list for this project because your wall will be different from ours. But you won't have any trouble making your own. (See "Shopping Tips," right.) After you establish how many bays you want, look at Figure A and count the parts. That'll give you a pretty accurate custom materials list for the project.

Choose the lengths of your 2x10s in multiples of 4 ft. That way, they'll join directly over the pegboard splices, and the horizontal 2x10 splices will be supported by the vertical 2x8s (Photo 4). That's

(continued on p. 199)

shopping tips!

➤ Buy 10-ft.-long 2x10s for the end frames. The final lengths are a few inches longer than 8 ft.

➤ Pick horizontal frames in 4-ft. increments: 8 ft. for two bays, 12 ft. for three bays, etc.

➤ Get one 4 x 8-ft. sheet of pegboard for each bay.

➤ Buy four 8-ft. 2x2s for each bay.

➤ When it comes to hardware, buy a 1-lb. box of 3-in. screws and a 1-lb. box of 1-1/2-in. washer-head screws. You'll have more than you need, but they'll come in handy someday.

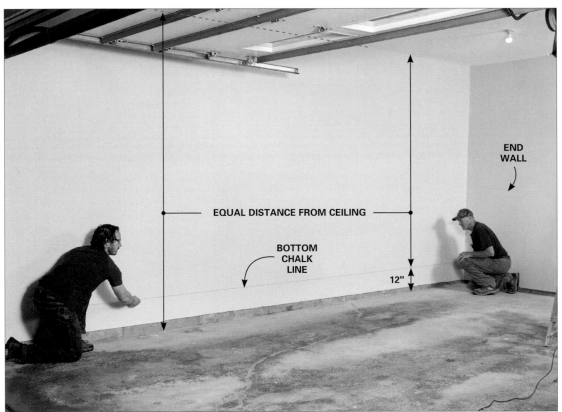

EQUAL DISTANCE FROM CEILING

END WALL

BOTTOM CHALK LINE

12"

1. Establish the bottom first. Measure up from the floor 12 in., then measure down to get the distance from the ceiling. Transfer that measurement to the other end of the wall and snap the bottom line for the base of the pegboard wall. Measure up from the bottom chalk line 93-1/8 in. and snap the top chalk line. Then snap horizontal lines spaced every 2 ft. from the top. Use a level to mark the stud centers and the other end of the wall.

2x2

2x10
END
FRAME

3"

1-1/2"

BLOCKING
BEHIND
DRYWALL

2. Begin framing at the end wall. Cut the two 2x10s to 99-1/8 in. long (one for each end). Center one above and below the top and bottom chalk lines and screw it to the corner blocking. There should be blocking extending at least 1 in. away from the corner. Center an 8-ft. 2x2 between the 2x10 ends, and screw it into place with 3-in. screws.

STUD
CENTER

MOUNTING
GRID

STUD
LOCATIONS

3. Build the grid work. Cut the horizontal 2x2s so they'll break in the middle of studs. Screw them to each stud with 3-in. screws using the chalk lines as a guide. Cut the last 2x2s 1-1/2 in. short of the end chalk line before fastening them to the studs. Then screw the last vertical 2x2 to the ends of each horizontal 2x2.

4. Build the 2x10 frame.
Center and screw the last vertical 2x10 to the end 2x2. Cut the horizontal 2x10s so any splices will fall over the 2x8 dividers. (Get a helper to support the boards for this part.) Then begin attaching the horizontal 2x10s to the end 2x10s and to the horizontal 2x2s with 3-in. screws.

2x10
HORIZONTAL
FRAME

5. Install the pegboard.
Cut the pegboard to length if needed, then rest it on the bottom 2x10 and screw it to the 2x2s with 1-1/4-in. washer-head screws, four per 2x2. (You'll see the 2x2s through the pegboard holes.) If needed, cut the last pegboard panel to width.

4' x 8'
PEGBOARD

(continued from p. 196)

why we used both 8- and 12-ft. 2x10s for the horizontal pieces. Joined together, they add up to our 20-ft. pegboard wall. Get one 8-ft. 2x8 for every two shelves (Photo 7). Here's a heads-up: 2x8s and 2x10s will be 1/8 to 1/2 in. over the stated lengths. So you'll have a little built-in fudge factor, but you may have to do a little trimming from time to time. Place shelf standards in any bays where you want adjustable shelves. Choose 6-ft. standards if they're available, and space them 1 ft. up from the bottom 2x10.

Paint before assembly

You'll spend as much time painting as you do building this system. We primed all the lumber, not only to provide a good base for the paint, but also to keep knots from eventually bleeding through the color coat. Then we rolled on two coats of latex wall paint, eggshell sheen.

A 3-in. roller frame with a 1/2-in.-nap sleeve works very well for all the painting. You can skip the paint tray and dip the sleeve right into the gallon paint can.

We used prefinished white pegboard—no painting needed. If you want to custom-paint unfinished pegboard, rough up the surface with 100-grit sandpaper, then prime and paint it the same way. But use a 1/4-in.-nap roller to ensure thin coats. If you use a thick-nap roller, the peg holes will likely

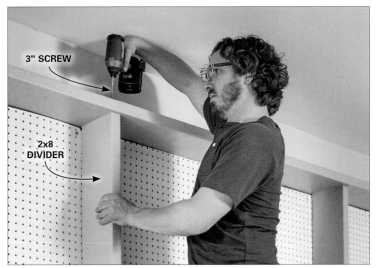

6. Add the dividers. Cut the 2x8 dividers to length, then center them over the pegboard seams. Plumb them with a 4-ft. level and screw them to the top and bottom 2x10s. Then toe-screw them to the horizontal 2x2s.

7. Screw in the shelf standards. Mount the standards on the dividers. Then cut the 2x8 shelves 1/4 in. shorter than the space between the standards and rest them on shelf standard brackets.

become plugged with paint. It took nearly a full gallon of paint to roll two coats over all the framing members.

Lay out the 2x2 mounting grid

Study Figure A to help you digest the following layout directions. Measure from the floor to make a mark at 12 in. (Photo 1). Then measure down from the ceiling to the mark and transfer it to the other end of the pegboard wall. (Garage floors are rarely level, but you can usually trust the ceiling.) Snap the bottom line. Measure up from the bottom line 93-1/8 in. to snap the top line. The 2x2s will go below the bottom line and above the top line to give you 96-1/8 in. outside to outside when they're in place.

If your pegboard will butt against a wall, install the 2x10 end frame first and measure from that to establish the 20-ft. 1/4-in. vertical grid line at the other end. (Or make the line to suit the number of bays you wish to have: 4 ft. 1/4 in., 8 ft. 1/4 in., etc.) Then snap horizontal lines spaced about every 2 ft. for the 2x2s that support the pegboard. Lastly, use a 4-ft. level to mark the end of the wall and the center of each stud (Photo 2).

8. Assemble the workbench frame. Build a 2x2 framework 24 in. deep and 2 in. narrower than the bay opening you intend to install it in.

9. Sheathe the top and bottom. Cover both sides with 1/2-in. particleboard. Use it to square the ladder as you glue and nail it to the 2x2s. Then add 1x3 edge banding to the bench edges.

10. Add the folding shelf brackets. Cut 27-in.-long 2x4 hinge supports and screw them through the pegboard into the 2x2s with 3-in. screws. Then attach the folding shelf brackets with 1-1/2-in. washer-head screws.

11. Attach the top from underneath. Rest the bench on the top, centered between the 2x8 uprights and 1/4 in. away from the pegboard, then screw it to the brackets from underneath with 1-1/2-in. washer-head screws.

Dealing with openings

Our expanse of plywood didn't include any windows, doors or electrical outlets or switches, but yours might. Surround windows with 2x10s just like you did with the perimeter. But beware of doors. Putting a 2x10 on the hinge side of a door means it'll open only 90 degrees. Experiment with the door swing to figure out which placement will work for you. If you have electrical boxes, you're required by code to install box extenders so the outlet or switch will be flush with the pegboard surface.

Sturdy, adjustable shelving

You can buy dedicated pegboard shelving brackets, but we wanted sturdy, adjustable 2x8 shelves, so we mounted 6-ft. shelf standards on most of the 2x8s (Photo 7). The 2x8s can span the full bay width without sagging. Unless you spend the time making all the bays exactly the same width, the shelf length will vary from one bay to the next.

Built-in, flip-up workbench

Our bench is 40 in. high and can be folded down into its own bay when you're not using it. The height is based on the pegboard wall base being located 1 ft. above the floor and the how-to steps shown in Photos 8–11. If you want a different height, you'll have to do some design work. But make sure to allow for a 1-1/2-in. gap between the bottom of the bench and the 2x10 when it's folded down. You'll need that gap for your fingers to safely open and close the bench.

You won't find these special folding shelf brackets in stores. Search online for "KV 16" Folding Shelf Bracket" and you'll find plenty of sources—and varying prices too! We paid about $65 with shipping for both. Make sure you get two.

Reconfigure as your needs change

Customize this storage system to suit your changing needs.

Flip-up workbench. Flip it up when you need it; fold it down when you don't.

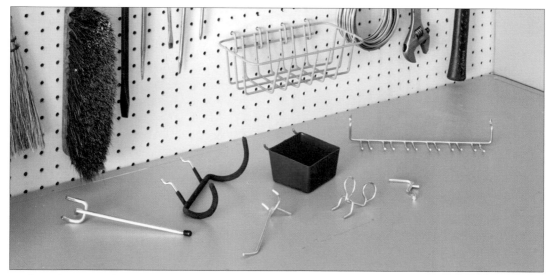

Pegboard accessories. Dozens of brackets are available to hang just about anything.

Dedicated storage. Install 2x4 backers to hold storage brackets and hooks.

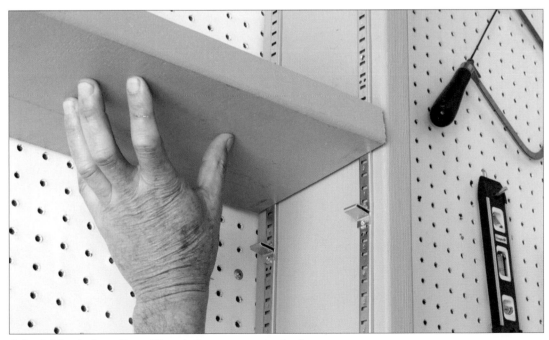

Adjustable shelves. Reposition shelves as your needs change.

PROFESSIONAL COST: $265

YOUR COST: $65

SAVINGS: $200

COMPLEXITY
Moderate

TOOLS
Table or circular saw
Jigsaw
Drill, 1/4-in. bit
Hand tools

MATERIALS
Plywood
Drawer slides
Aluminum rod
Brad nails

Super-useful kitchen rollout

It's always a challenge to find matching food storage containers and lids. This rollout solves the problem by keeping them all neatly organized and easily accessible. The full-extension drawer slides are the key. To simplify tricky drawer slide installation, we've designed an ingenious carrier system that allows you to mount the slides and make sure everything is working smoothly before the rollout is mounted in the cabinet.

Tools and materials

Our 24-in. base cabinet required a 4 x 4-ft. sheet of 1/2-in.-thick plywood for the rollout, plus a 2 x 3-ft. scrap of 3/4-in. plywood for the carrier. Yours may require more or less. We found high-quality birch plywood at a home center for this project. If you have trouble finding nice plywood, consider ordering Baltic birch or ApplePly plywood from a home center or local lumberyard. The carrier fits under the rollout and isn't very conspicuous, so almost any flat piece of 3/4-in. plywood will work for that.

In addition to the lumber, you'll need a pair of 22-in. full-extension ball-bearing slides and a 1/4-in. aluminum rod.

We used a table saw to cut the plywood parts, but if you're careful to make accurate cuts, a circular saw will work. You'll need a jigsaw with a plywood-cutting blade to cut the curves on the sides and dividers. We used a finish nail gun and 1-1/4-in.-long brad nails to connect the parts, but you could substitute trim-head screws if you don't mind the larger holes they leave.

Measure the base cabinet

Most base cabinets are about 23 in. deep and will accommodate this rollout, but measure yours to be sure. If the measurement from the back of the face frame to the back of the cabinet is less than 22 in., you'll have to build a shallower rollout and use shorter drawer slides.

The other critical measurement is the width. Measure the clear opening width; that is, the width from any protruding hinge or door parts to the opposite side of the cabinet opening (Photo 1). Subtract 3 in. from this measurement to determine the width of parts B, C, D and E.

OPENING WIDTH

1. Measure the opening. Measure from any protruding hinges or door parts to the opposite side to find the opening width. Also check to make sure the cabinet is at least 22 in. deep.

Cut out the parts

After adjusting the size of parts B, C, D and E for the cabinet width, you can cut out all the parts except the carrier bottom. If you're using a table saw, make partial cuts to form the L-shaped sides. But remember, you can't see how far the blade is cutting on the underside, so be sure to stop short of your inside corner marks by at least an inch. Photo 2 shows how to complete the cut with a jigsaw.

Trace along the edge of a 1-gallon paint can to draw the radius for the curve on the side panels. Trace along a quart-size can to draw the radius on the dividers. Cut the curves on the sides and dividers with a jigsaw (Photo 3). Smooth the curved cuts with 100-grit sandpaper.

Build the rollout

Mark the location of the 1/4-in. rod on the side panels using Figure A as a guide. Wrap tape around a 1/4-in. drill bit 1/4 in. from the end to use as a depth guide while drilling. Drill 1/4-in.-deep holes at the marks. Use a hacksaw to cut an aluminum rod 1/2 in. longer than the width of the bottom.

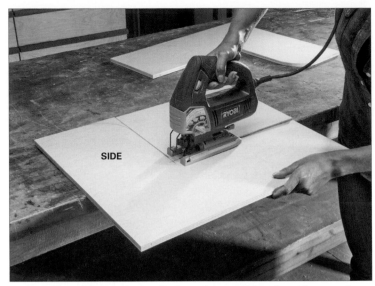

2. Cut the side panels. Cut each panel to size. Then cut the notch to form the L-shape. Start with a table saw or circular saw for the straight cuts. Finish the inside corner with a jigsaw.

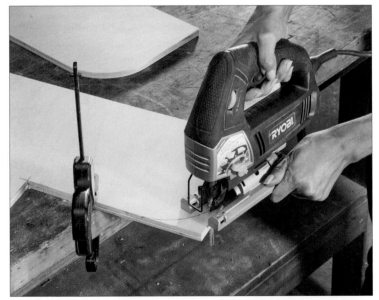

3. Cut the curves. Mark the curves on the side panels by tracing along a gallon paint can. Mark the dividers using a quart-size paint can. Then cut with a jigsaw.

Figure A

Food storage container rollout

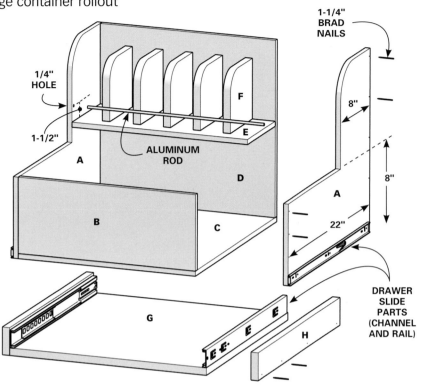

1-1/4" BRAD NAILS

1/4" HOLE

1-1/2"

ALUMINUM ROD

8"

8"

22"

DRAWER SLIDE PARTS (CHANNEL AND RAIL)

A, B, C, D, E, F, G, H

Cutting List

KEY	QTY.	MATERIAL	DIMENSIONS	PART
A	2	1/2" plywood	1/2" x 22" x 18"	Sides
B	1	1/2" plywood	1/2" x 7-1/2" x 18"	Front
C	1	1/2" plywood	1/2" x 22" x 18"	Bottom
D	1	1/2" plywood	1/2" x 17-1/2" x 18"	Back
E	1	1/2" plywood	1/2" x 7-1/2" x 18"	Shelf
F	5*	1/2" plywood	1/2" x 6" x 6"	Dividers
G	1	3/4" plywood	3/4" x 20" x 22"	Carrier bottom
H	2	3/4" plywood	3/4" x 2-3/4" x 22"	Carrier sides

Note: These sizes are for a 24-in.-wide base cabinet. To fit your cabinet, adjust the sizes according to the instructions on p. 205.

Materials List

ITEM	QTY.
1/2" x 4' x 4' plywood	1
3/4" x 2' x 3' plywood	1
Pair of 22" full-extension slides	1
36" x 1/4" aluminum rod	1
Small package of 1-1/4" brad nails	1

Apply wood glue to all edges that meet, and arrange the sides, bottom, front and back on a workbench and clamp them together. Work the aluminum rod into the holes. Tap the parts with a hammer to align the edges perfectly before connecting them with brad nails (Photo 4). Take your time aiming the nail gun to avoid nail blowouts.

Finish the rollout by adding the dividers. First decide how many dividers you want and calculate the width of the space between the dividers. Cut a spacer block to that dimension and use it as a guide to install the dividers. Attach the dividers to the shelf (Photo 5). Then measure down 7-1/2 in. from the top and make marks to indicate the top edge of the divider shelf. Line up the divider assembly with these marks and nail it in. Draw divider center lines on the back of the rollout as a nailing guide. Then attach the dividers (Photo 6).

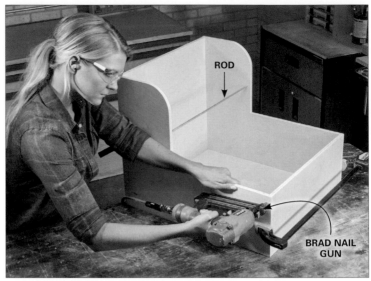

4. Assemble the rollout. Glue and clamp the parts together. Don't forget to install the rod. Align the edges by tapping on the panels with your hand or a hammer. Then nail the parts together.

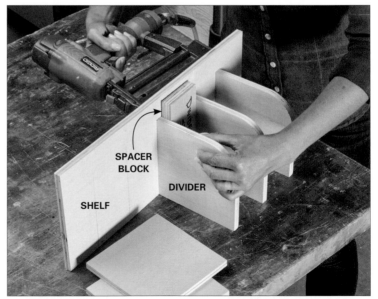

5. Nail the dividers to the shelf. Cut a spacer the width of the desired space between dividers and use it to position the dividers as you nail them to the shelf.

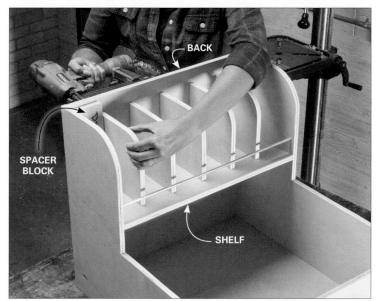

BACK

SPACER BLOCK

SHELF

6. **Nail the dividers to the rollout.** Position the shelf and nail through the sides into the shelf. Then use the spacer block to align the dividers and nail through the back.

DRAWER SLIDE RAIL

7. **Screw the drawer slide to the rollout.** Separate the drawer slides and attach the rail to the rollout. Align the rail flush to the bottom and flush to the front before driving the screws.

Drawer slides require 1/2-in. clearance on each side, so making the carrier exactly 1 in. wider than the rollout will result in a perfect fit. Measure the width of the completed rollout and add exactly 1 in. to determine the width of the carrier bottom. Cut the carrier bottom from 3/4-in. plywood. Then screw the carrier sides to the carrier bottom to prepare the carrier for mounting the drawer slides.

Mount the slides

Follow the instructions included with your drawer slides to separate the slides into two parts: a channel and a rail. Usually, pressing down on a plastic lever releases the parts and allows you to separate them. Screw the rails to the drawer (Photo 7) and the channels to the carrier sides (Photo 8).

When you're done installing the slides, check the fit by carefully aligning the rails with the channels and sliding them together. The rollout should glide easily on the ball-bearing slides. If the slides seem too tight, you can adjust the fit by removing one of the carrier sides and slipping a thin cardboard shim between the carrier side and carrier bottom before reassembling them.

Mount the rollout in the cabinet

Photo 9 shows fitting the carrier assembly into the cabinet. There will be a little side-to-side play, so you can adjust the position to clear the hinge and door. This will probably require you to offset the carrier slightly away from the hinge side. Screw the carrier to the bottom of the cabinet and you're ready to install the rollout (Photo 10). Since you've already checked the fit, it should operate perfectly. Now load it up with containers and lids and enjoy your neatly organized container rollout.

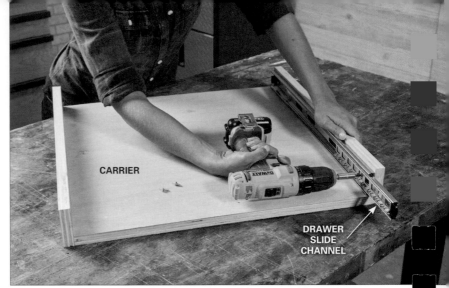

CARRIER

DRAWER SLIDE CHANNEL

8. Screw the drawer slide channel to the carrier. Rest the drawer slide channel on the carrier and align the front flush to the front of the carrier side.

9. Install the carrier. Position the carrier so that the rollout will clear any hinge or door parts. Drive screws through the carrier bottom into the cabinet.

10. **Install the rollout**. Line up the rails and channels and slide the rollout into the cabinet. Slide it back and forth a few times to make sure it rolls smoothly.

Cabinet door rack

All that wide open space under the sink is a black hole for cleaning products, dish scrubbers, trash bags—you name it. If you're tired of exploring its depths every time you need something, build this handy door-mounted shelf. Better than store-bought wire racks, it mounts securely, has the same wood finish as your cabinet and maximizes space because you custom-fit it for your cabinet.

This shelf is made from standard 1x4 lumber (which is 3/4 in. x 3-1/2 in.). If you have access to a table saw and have a drill, screwdriver, some wood glue and a tape measure, you can build this project. It takes only a few hours.

The shelf has a unique built-in system (Photos 6 and 7) to make mounting it to the back side of a cabinet door a snap. The shelf gets screwed into the solid wood stiles of the door (not into the panel).

Sizing tips

Because there's no standard size for sink base cabinets, here are a few tips to help you size your door-mounted shelf. Measure the height and width of the cabinet opening (Photo 1). The shelf unit must be 1/2 in. less in height and 2 in. less in width (not including the mounting ears shown in Photo 6). These measurements ensure that the shelf unit will clear the frame by 1/4 in. on all sides as you close the cabinet

1. Measure the cabinet opening (height and width) to size the door rack.

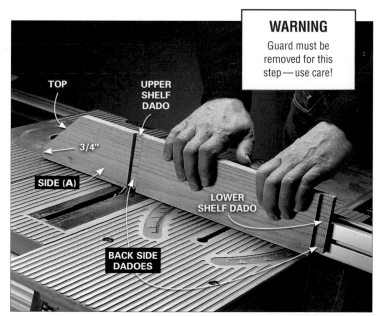

WARNING
Guard must be removed for this step—use care!

2. Cut the sides (A) to length, then cut the dadoes in the sides and back of each side. See text for dimensions.

door. Here's how to size each part:

- ➤ The height of the 3-1/2-in.-deep sides (A) must be 1/2 in. shorter than the height of the opening.

- ➤ The 3-1/4-in.-deep shelves (B) are cut 3 in. shorter than the width of the opening. These pieces are ripped 1/4 in. thinner than the side to allow space for gluing the mounting strips (C) to the back side of the shelves (Photo 4).

- ➤ The 1/4-in. x 3/4-in. mounting strips must be 2-1/2 in. longer than B or 1/2 in. shorter than the width of the door opening.

Preparing the sides

After measuring the opening's height and width, cut the sides (A) to length. Then cut a 45-degree taper on the tops of each piece, leaving 3/4 in. at the top as shown in Photo 2. Label the inside of each side so you don't cut the dado (groove) for each shelf on the wrong side. Notice that there are two 1/4-in. notches on the back edge of each side (Photo 2) to accept the mounting strips (C).

To cut the dadoes, set your table saw blade so it's 1/4 in. high. Mark the locations of each dado. The lower dado is on the bottom of the sides, and the top of the upper shelf is 13-1/2 in. from the bottom of the sides.

Cut the dadoes in the inner sides of A, using your miter

WARNING
Guard removed for photo—use yours.

RAILS (D)

MOUNTING STRIPS (C)

3. Rip the mounting strips (C) and the rails (D) from 1x4 lumber.

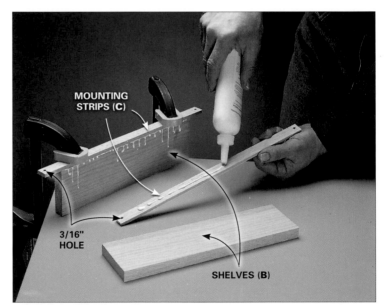

MOUNTING STRIPS (C)

3/16" HOLE

SHELVES (B)

4. Glue mounting strips (C) to the back side of the shelves. Drill holes in the mounting strips before assembling.

gauge as a guide to push the workpiece through the saw. Our table saw has an extra-wide miter gauge for stability. If your table saw has a small miter gauge, screw a piece of wood to its front edge to extend it to within 1/4 in. of the saw blade. You could make the dado cut in one pass with a special dado blade, but if you don't have one, just make repeated cuts (Photo 2) with a standard blade.

Making the shelves

Cut the shelves (B) to length from 1x4, then rip them to a width of 3-1/4 in. Make the 1/4-in. x 3/4-in. mounting strips (C) and front rails (D) by ripping them from a wider piece as shown in Photo 3.

Before you glue these pieces to the backs of the shelves (Photo 4), drill a 3/16-in. hole 3/8 in. from each end. You'll use these holes later to mount the shelf to the door stiles.

Assembly

Lay out the sides face down as shown in Photo 5. Now, slip the shelves with the mounting strips attached into the dadoes and make sure they fit snugly.

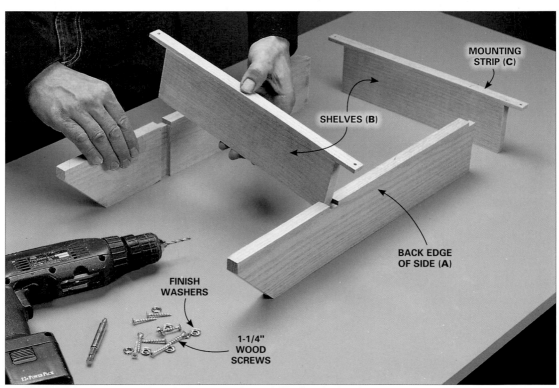

MOUNTING STRIP (C)

SHELVES (B)

BACK EDGE OF SIDE (A)

FINISH WASHERS

1-1/4" WOOD SCREWS

5. Slip the shelves into the dado cuts. Then drill pilot holes into the sides of A and screw the shelves in place with 1-1/4-in. wood screws and finish washers.

pro tips!

> ➤ You can also modify this design to work in other cabinets for holding spices, canned goods or craft supplies.

Drill pilot holes for the screws (3/4 in. from the front and back of A) through the sides into the shelves. Use 1-1/4-in. wood screws with finish washers to secure the shelves to the sides.

To finish the assembly, flip the shelves and sides face-up. Cut the 1/4-in. x 3/4-in. front rails (D) to length, drill pilot holes and fasten them (Photo 6) to the front of the sides. We chose to put the lower rail 2 in. up from the bottom shelf and the upper rail 1-1/2 in. up from the upper

shelf. These heights work fine for most products and allow you to pull things out instead of lifting them each time. You can always add a second rail just above if needed.

Mounting to the door

Before mounting the unit to the door, apply masking tape to the inside of the door as shown in Photo 7. Close the door and mark the cabinet opening on the tape with a pencil from the inside. This will guide you when you're

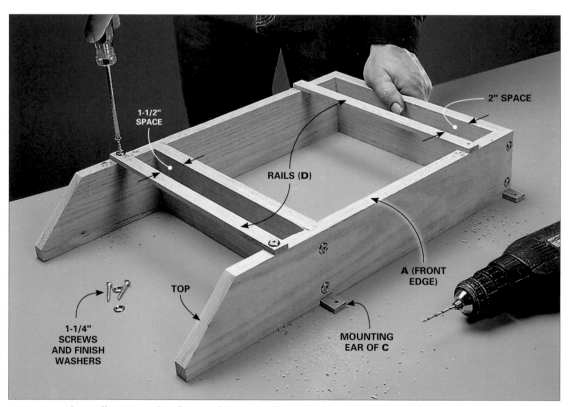

6. Fasten the rails (D) to the front of the shelf assembly. Drill pilot holes and use 1-1/4-in. wood screws and finish washers.

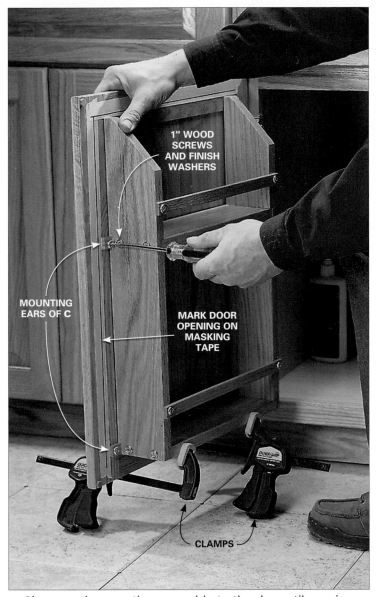

1" WOOD
SCREWS
AND FINISH
WASHERS

MOUNTING
EARS OF C

MARK DOOR
OPENING ON
MASKING
TAPE

CLAMPS

7. Clamp and screw the assembly to the door stiles using 1-in. wood screws and finish washers.

CAUTION

If you have small children, be sure that cabinets containing cleaning products have child-proof latches attached.

mounting the shelf to the door. Mount the shelf 1/4 in. from the top mark you made on the tape, and align the ear of the mounting strip 1/4 in. from the opening mark on the door. Mark the holes from the mounting strips onto the door and drill pilot holes for the screws. Be careful not to drill through the door! Screw the assembly to the door (Photo 7) using No. 8 x 1-in. screws and finish washers.

Because of the added weight of the shelf and the products, some doors with self-closing hinges may not snap closed as easily as before. To remedy this, you may need to install an extra hinge centered between the other two, or add a magnetic catch at the top of the door.

Remove the shelf from the door, sand it with 150-grit sandpaper, then apply varnish. Shown here are several coats of a clear lacquer spray available at hardware stores. Always apply lacquer in a well-ventilated area away from any pilot flames.

Play It Safe

Ladder safety

Ever climbed halfway up an extension ladder and felt it sliding out from beneath your feet? You quickly realize you should have spent a few more minutes making sure the ladder feet were solidly set before starting your climb. Climbing a ladder can be safe, even under the less-than-perfect situations you find around your home. We'll show some easy ways to provide solid footing and a stable top to avoid heart-stopping experiences.

Secure the feet

In addition to establishing a level base, make sure the feet can't slip backward. On soft ground, flip up the ladder shoes so the spurs poke into the ground (left photo on p. 223). On decks, it's a simple matter to screw down a cleat (photo below). Before you set up the ladder on hard surfaces, clean the bottom of the ladder feet and sweep away sand and dirt that could cause the ladder to slip.

If it still seems like the ladder could slip, tie ropes to both ladder legs beneath the lowest rung and tie the other end of the ropes to a solidly anchored object at or near the base of the wall.

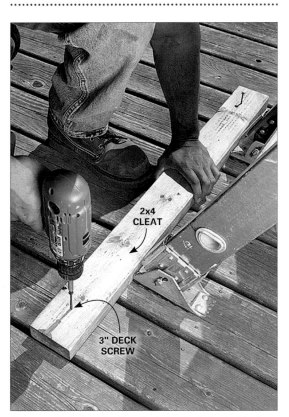

2x4 CLEAT

3" DECK SCREW

Screw a 2x4 cleat to the deck behind the ladder's feet to prevent the ladder from slipping backward.

Get the angle right

Setting the ladder at the correct angle is one of the most important steps to a safe ladder setup. Too steep and it could tip over backward. Too much angle and it could bend or the bottom could slide out. The photo shows how to get the angle just right. If an obstacle prevents you from setting the ladder at the correct angle, don't take chances—consider using methods like scaffolding instead.

EXTEND ARMS

PALMS TOUCH RUNG

LADDER AT CORRECT ANGLE

TOUCH TOES TO LADDER BASE

Set your ladder at the correct angle. Put your toes against the ladder's feet. Stand straight up and extend your arms. The palms of your hands should just reach the ladder's rung.

Tie the top for extra security

If you plan to make several trips up and down while the ladder is in the same location, it pays to secure the top to keep it from sliding. This is especially important if you'll be stepping onto a roof (photo below). Ties will prevent the ladder from sliding sideways as you step to and from the roof. Using the setup we show has the added advantage of protecting the edge of the shingles. It will only take a few minutes to screw the two eye screws into a 2x4 and the 2x4 to the fascia board. You can keep the rig handy for future use. You'll be left with a few small screw holes in the fascia, but that's a small price to pay for this extra measure of security.

Here are a few more tips for steadying the top of the ladder. If you have a choice, set up the ladder where there's an adjoining wall, chimney or other structure to hold it in place. Also, if you regularly set the ladder against the same location on your metal gutters, add extra gutter straps to strengthen the gutter in the area where the ladder top rests. Then install eye screws out of sight above the gutter to provide anchors for securing your ladder with rope or wire.

Secure the top against a wall

Providing a stable base is only half the battle. You also have to make sure the top of the ladder can't slide when the rails rest against a wall. Make sure the ladder is vertical and the top is resting on an even surface. Angling the ladder to the left or right to reach a remote spot is asking for trouble.

There are a couple of add-on accessories that help stabilize the top of ladders. The first is a pair of rubber or soft plastic "mitts" (available at hardware stores and home centers) that slip over the top of the ladder's rails. They provide a better grip on the siding and protect it from ladder damage. Ladder stabilizers are another great add-on accessory (photo below). The large rubber pads grip almost any surface to keep the top from slipping sideways and help spread out the load to prevent damage to fragile siding materials like vinyl or aluminum. Stabilizers also span window openings and hold the ladder away from the building to allow work on gutters and overhangs. Ladders and stabilizers and are available almost everywhere ladders are sold. We highly recommend them for any kind of extensive work, such as washing and painting.

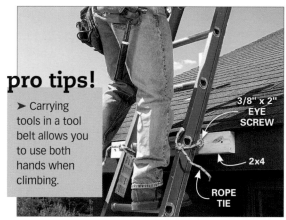

pro tips!

➤ Carrying tools in a tool belt allows you to use both hands when climbing.

3/8" x 2" EYE SCREW

2x4

ROPE TIE

Secure the top of your ladder by tying it to a solid anchor. Make a reusable anchoring rig by screwing two 3/8-in. x 2-in. eye screws into a 32-in. length of 2x4. Then screw the 2x4 to the fascia with 3-in. deck screws.

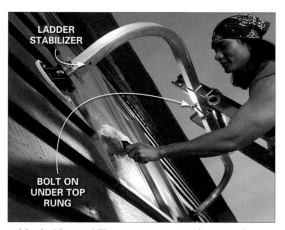

LADDER STABILIZER

BOLT ON UNDER TOP RUNG

Add a ladder stabilizer accessory to the top of your ladder to span windows and to provide extra stability. Follow the stabilizer installation instructions carefully.

Provide a level base

Even with the ladder at the correct angle, it can still tip sideways if the feet aren't level with each other and on solid ground.

It's unsafe to stack boards, bricks or other stuff under one of the feet to level the ladder. Instead, scrape out a shallow trench under the high-side foot (photo below). The claw of a hammer is perfect for this task, and it's almost always handy.

If digging is impractical because your site is steeply sloped, or you want to set the ladder on stairs or some other uneven, hard surface, don't opt for a makeshift solution. Instead, buy adjustable leg-leveling extensions that bolt onto the bottom of your ladder. You'll use them often if you live on a sloped lot. To see what's available, check the ladder manufacturer's website or a store that sells your ladder brand.

MOVE LADDER BACK

SHOES FLIPPED UP

SPUR

DIG UNDER HIGH SIDE

FOOT IN HOLE

FOOT ON GROUND

Dig a trench under the high-side foot when your ladder is on uneven ground. Flip the shoes up when you're setting up the ladder on soft ground. The spurs will dig in and prevent the ladder from slipping.

Jump on the lowest rung to set the ladder firmly and to test for stability. If the ladder tips to one side, move it aside and adjust the depth of the hole.

How to haul stuff safely

How many times have you seen coolers, lamps or sofa cushions lying in the road? All of this stuff flying off trucks can be a real hazard for motorists and a hassle for you if you're the one losing something valuable. Securing truckloads is easy if you get the right gear. The products shown here can help you secure those loads, whether you're hauling building materials or a motocross bike, or just spending a day at the beach.

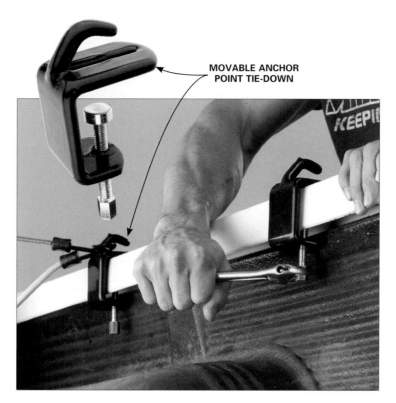

MOVABLE ANCHOR
POINT TIE-DOWN

Solid tie-downs are a must

These movable clamp-style tie-downs mount anywhere along your truck's box and clamp tightly to the side rails. You can position and remove them quickly with a socket wrench or socket. As with all clamp-type accessories, check them for tightness after the first half hour of traveling. Available at auto parts stores and realtruck.com.

Cargo ramps help you roll heavy items

Each aluminum ramp end outfitted with a sturdy yellow pine or Douglas fir 2x8 or 2x10 will hold up to 700 lbs. (no big motorcycles). This works great for light motorbikes and wheelbarrows of dirt or mulch. "Ramparts" are available at auto parts stores and jcwhitney.com.

ALUMINUM RAMP END WITH BOLTS

2x8 DOUGLAS FIR OR YELLOW PINE

Quick-release straps

Heavy-duty, quick-release straps are available in a variety of lengths, sizes and tensile strengths. Flexible bungee cords work well for light-duty stuff but will stretch and fail if you're trying to secure heavy objects. An adjustable tie-down strap that you can cinch tight will keep a load from shifting and toppling. Choose one with a tensile strength at least twice the weight of your total load. Go to jcwhitney.com or choose others at home centers or auto parts stores.

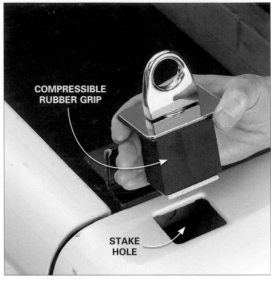

COMPRESSIBLE
RUBBER GRIP

STAKE
HOLE

TIE-DOWN
STRAP

QUICK-
RELEASE
CLAMP

Stake hole tie-downs

Just push stake hole tie-downs into the stake hole and then turn the loop clockwise to compress the rubber insert. Give them several turns and then a yank to make sure they're snug. Check them again after traveling awhile and retighten them if necessary. Available at jcwhitney.com.

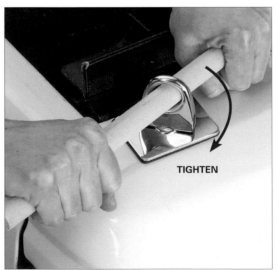

TIGHTEN

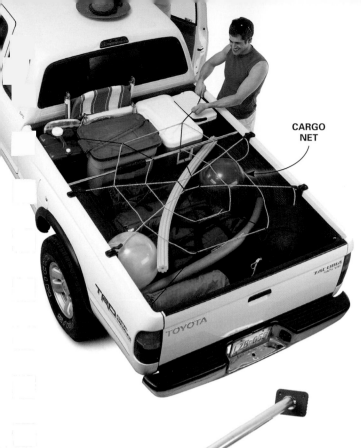

CARGO NET

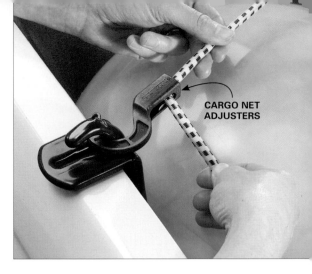

CARGO NET ADJUSTERS

Cargo nets

Cargo nets are perfect for keeping light items like cushions, inflated toys and chairs from flying out of the box. This type has eight fastening locations, and each hook has a built-in adjuster to secure the load to your liking. Find cargo nets at auto parts stores and jcwhitney.com.

CARGO BAR SQUEEZE ADJUSTER

Quick-release cargo bars

Quick-release cargo bars keep boxes and coolers from sliding around in the pickup box. They'll adjust for small or large pickup boxes and ratchet tight with the squeeze of a trigger. The bars work great for keeping boxed or bagged items (even groceries) right behind the cab and out of the wind. Available at most auto parts stores and northerntool.com.

How to safely work alone

Working alone isn't much fun, especially when you're trying to do the work of two. No one's around to hold the other end of the tape, support the other end of the board, or hand tools or materials up to the roof. And to top it all off, there's no one to visit with either.

We can't help you with the loneliness (get a dog), but we can offer some commonsense tips to make solo work as painless and productive as possible. The idea is to creatively use clamps, blocks, nails, sawhorses and scrap building materials in new, different ways. Once you start thinking like this, you'll be surprised at how much you can accomplish by yourself.

CHAIN

BLOCK

Levers will give you more lifting power than a burly neighbor

Lever posts out of the ground by wrapping a chain around the base of the post and slipping a long plank through the chain. Pry against a block resting on the ground to keep the lever from digging into the soil. Sometimes you'll have to excavate around the tops of stubborn concrete-embedded posts to remove some of the dirt trapping the top of the concrete.

Snap chalk lines when you lack a third hand

Everyone knows how to pound in a nail to hold the end of a chalk line when they're alone, but what do you do on a basement floor? You use a brick to anchor it down, that's what. That's simple, but here's another trick that's a little tougher to master. When you have less-than-4-ft. snaps and you don't want to fool with or damage the surface with a nail, learn how to snap lines by holding the handle on the chalk box with the line extended past the mark. Hold the line tight and tip the box down so you can pluck the line with your thumb and index finger.

HOLD HANDLE WITH RING FINGER; PLUCK STRING WITH THUMB AND INDEX FINGER

Handle long, awkward pieces with clamps, blocks, screws and nails

The toughest solo jobs are holding up a full sheet of plywood, supporting the top row of drywall, and securing strips of siding or long boards in exactly the right position while you fasten them. Sometimes you can stick a clamp somewhere to support long boards, nail in a block directly below the work or even pound in a couple of nails to rest the two bottom corners of plywood sheathing while you fine-tune the placement and do the fastening.

Occasionally you'll need to place fasteners through finished surfaces, but don't sweat it. Nails leave relatively small, fixable holes and drywall screw holes are nearly invisible. These little insults are pretty tame compared with the mess you can have with a falling cabinet that you're trying to hold up while fastening!

Big, cumbersome cabinets are easy to hang alone if you first screw a level 1x4 through the wall into the studs at the right height. Then you can rest the cabinet while you fasten it to the wall. Holding 10-ft. gutter sections for fastening is a hassle. But support the far end with a clamp attached to the bottom of the fascia and it's painless (photo below).

Listen to the music

Find circuit breakers by plugging a loud radio into the outlet you're working on. You'll know you have the right circuit breaker when the music dies. But don't assume the electricity is off in all the other outlets or lights in the room. Before doing any wiring, plug the radio into other outlets you plan to work on. Some duplex outlets can have different circuits running to adjacent outlets. To be safe, test both the top and bottom with the radio. For lights, turn the light switch on and off to be sure.

NEW GUTTER

CLAMPS ON FASCIA BOARD

Use pivot points and balance to wrestle long ladders

More broken windows and injuries happen from raising, lowering and moving ladders around than actually using them. The longer the ladder, the harder it is to control. Here's how to handle the longest ladders alone.

Anchor the feet of extension ladders against the base of the building and "walk" the ladder up to raise it. The solid wall keeps the feet from kicking out as the ladder's raised. To lower ladders, move the feet back against the building and reverse the process.

ANCHOR FEET AGAINST HOUSE

WARNING
Stay away from power lines.

1. Anchor the base and walk the ladder up.

HEAVY WEIGHT ANCHORS FEET

2. Extend the ladder while holding it vertical.

3. Roll the top to walk the ladder sideways.

Use balance and grip to haul heavy plywood

Lift sheet goods by placing one hand under the sheet, slightly in front of center, and your other hand at the top, slightly behind the center. Hoist it so that the middle of the sheet rests on the ball of your shoulder. Your shoulder and back handle the bulk of the weight while your hands only need to balance it. Bonus: You'll be able to see where you're going, thread through doorways and even navigate up and down stairs.

....

1. Pull it out flat.

2. Grip it top and bottom and lift with your legs.

3. Balance it and carry it away.

2x12s

BLOCKS TO KEEP LEGS FROM SINKING

HEAVY-DUTY SAWHORSES

Using sturdy sawhorses and 2x12s is safer and more productive than reaching from ladders

Working alone on ladders can be inefficient and dangerous, especially because you'll be tempted to over-extend your reach and carry too many tools, paint cans, shingles or lumber when no one is on hand to pass you things. Nothing speeds up high, solo work like the spacious elevated work platform scaffolding provides. You'll be able to keep materials and tools at arm's length and safely reach a wide area without constantly moving ladders.

The scaffolding doesn't have to be anything fancy. When you have a job less than 10 ft. from the ground, set a couple of solid, crack-free, 2x12 boards (avoid large knots) over a pair of sturdy sawhorses for a platform you can move around on. Just make sure your setup is on even ground to keep the horses from collapsing, and avoid "walking the plank" by remembering that there are no safety rails. Keep plank ends close to sawhorses or they'll flip up when you step on the ends, like they do in slapstick movies (only it won't be nearly as funny in real life).

For higher jobs, like painting second-floor eaves or replacing windows or siding, go to the rental store and examine your scaffolding options. You can rent long, lightweight aluminum planks with various styles of jacks to support them and the same platform "section style" scaffolding you see the pros use on big construction sites. Tell the scaffolding supplier about the job you're planning to do and how high you'll be working to get help choosing the best scaffold. Most scaffolding can be carried in a pickup, but rental stores will deliver too. You'll forgive the cost when you see how your productivity increases.

Extend your saw table with 2x4s and plywood

It's not always easy to find a willing helper to hold up long boards when you're ripping on the table saw. Here's a setup that you can rig in just a few minutes.

Lay 2x4s perpendicular to sawhorses to support the lips of the saw table. Screw the 2x4s to the tops of the sawhorses. Lay a sheet of plywood directly behind the saw and lock it in place with 1-5/8 in. drywall screws.

PLYWOOD SCREWED TO 2x4s

2x4s SCREWED TO SAWHORSE

SAW TABLE RESTS ON 2x4s

Start nails or screws before hoisting the load

How many times have you tried to hold a board or sheet of material in place and start a nail or screw? When hanging drywall, plywood or even a rim joist (the board that ties a whole bunch of joist ends together), mark the framing locations and tack a few fasteners in the material before hoisting it. Then you can hold it with one hand while driving in the fasteners.

PRESTARTED NAILS

Use a lever and fulcrum to ease the awkwardness of solitary door hanging

Hang doors back onto hinges by levering the door into position with a 1x4 fulcrumed on a 3/4-in. block of wood. Line up the top hinge leaves, slip in the top hinge pin and then line up the other two leaves and drop in the other pins.

PRY BAR

BLOCK FOR HIGHER DOORS

On the following pages, the repair experts below provide examples of repairs they make that frankly are so simple that they feel bad charging for them. Many of the fixes they suggest are simple things that you may have just overlooked. Other solutions are less obvious. Of course, there are times when you must rely on the pros to get the job done. But if you follow the advice here, you may be able to save a big chunk of change the next time something goes wrong.

Les Zell

Les, the owner of Zell Plumbing and Heating, got his start in the U.S. Navy Construction Battalion. Then he went on to become a journeyman and finally a master plumber.

Costas Stavrou

Costas graduated from technical college with a degree in refrigeration, air conditioning and major appliance repair. He has run his own company, CSG Repair, since 1982.

Al Hildenbrand

Al has a bachelor of science degree in electrical engineering and a master electrician's license. An electrical contractor for 30 years, he has his own company, Al's Electric Works.

Bob Schmahl

Bob has 42 years' experience in the heating and air conditioning business. He worked as a journeyman until he got his Master Warm Air Venting & Heating license in 1987.

Before you call a plumber

"You'd be surprised how often we get calls complaining about no water or a lack of pressure, and then show up to discover something simple like a water valve that's shut off or a plugged faucet aerator." – **Les Zell**

PILOT FLAME
SHOULD BE
HERE

GAS WATER
HEATER

No hot water? Check the pilot light

Les says you'd be surprised how often he has to charge for a service call just to relight a water heater pilot light. So before you call the plumber, remove the metal cover located at the bottom of the water heater or simply look through the glass door to see if the pilot is lit. If you don't see a small pilot light flame, follow the instructions for relighting the pilot on the label pasted to the tank. Some high-efficiency water heaters don't have a pilot light that stays lit all the time. If you have one of these, check your owner's manual before you reach for your phone.

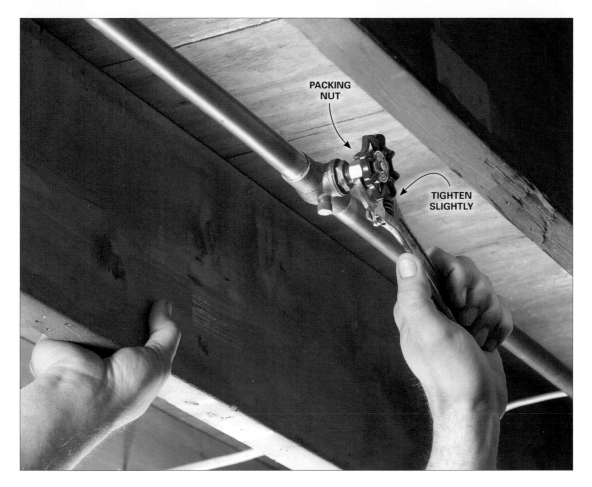

PACKING NUT

TIGHTEN SLIGHTLY

Got a leak?

Plumbers say that leaks are one of the most common complaints they get. Valves are one of the main culprits because they have moving parts and seals that can wear out. The next time you see a suspicious puddle of water, look for a leaky valve before you call the plumber. Look at the valve to see if water is leaking out around the valve stem. If it is, try turning the packing nut (photo above) about an eighth turn with a wrench. You'll know if you overtighten the nut because the valve will be hard to turn. If tightening the nut doesn't stop the leak, the fix is a little tougher. You'll have to shut off the main water valve, remove the handle and nut, and add to or replace the packing material—still a pretty easy fix.

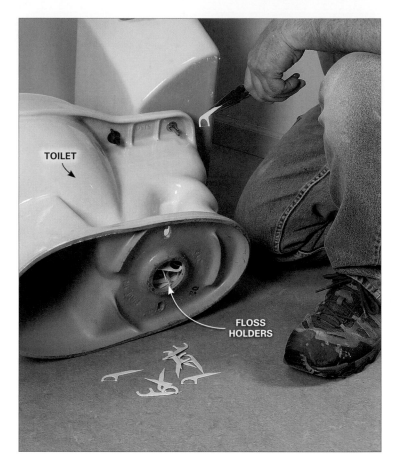

TOILET

FLOSS
HOLDERS

"Your toilet's not a garbage can"

Les got a call to unplug a toilet he had recently installed. He was surprised because he had put in a toilet that he knew was almost impossible to clog. After repeated attempts with a plunger and a toilet auger, he gave up and removed the toilet to look in from the bottom. The outlet was completely clogged with a tangled web of plastic dental floss holders, which had to be removed one at a time with needle-nose pliers. Save yourself a service call. Use the wastebasket for garbage.

FAUCET AERATOR

Low water pressure at the faucet?

Over time, aerators get clogged with minerals or other bits of stuff that break loose from the inside of the pipes. Remove the aerator by turning it clockwise when you're looking down on it. You may have to grip it with pliers to unscrew it. Once it's off, you can take the parts out of the aerator and clean them, but it's usually better to simply replace it. Take it along to the hardware store to find an exact thread match.

Before you call for an appliance repair

"The No. 1 thing for all appliances is to check the power first. In other words, is the breaker off, or did someone unplug the appliance to plug in a drill or something. Seriously, it's happened a million times. I'll go over there, plug in the appliance and say I'm really sorry, but I'll still have to charge you."— **Costas Stavrou**

COIL CLEANING BRUSH

DIRTY REFRIGERATOR COILS

Refrigerator not cooling?

It could be as simple as turning the dial to a cooler setting. Check the controls. Costas says it's not uncommon to find that the refrigerator controls are set wrong. Someone may have bumped the dial while putting away the milk or an inquisitive toddler may have twisted the knob.

Cooling coils completely caked with pet hair and dust are also incredibly common. Remove the front grille and vacuum the coils.

Water coming out of the dishwasher?

Costas says a leak, and an unusual whooshing sound coming from the dishwasher, are sure signs that someone used regular dishwashing liquid rather than dishwasher detergent, which is low sudsing. Costas squirts a bit of defoaming solution, typically used in carpet shampoo machines, into the dishwasher. But you can rinse all of the detergent from the dishwasher by repeatedly adding a gallon of water and running the dishwasher on the drain cycle.

Is your freezer full of frost?

That's a sure sign that the freezer door is ajar. All it takes is one too many cartons of ice cream to hold the door open a crack. Rearrange the freezer contents so the door closes completely and you may save $100 on a service call.

Washer not filling?

When Costas gets a call about a washing machine that's not filling with water, the first thing he asks is whether the water valves leading to the machine are open. If your washer isn't filling, check to make sure the water is on before you call for service.

IGNITER

BURNER

No flame at the burners?

➤ If you don't hear gas coming out when the burner is turned on, gas isn't getting to the stove. Check to make sure the gas is turned on.

➤ If you hear gas coming out but the burner won't light, make sure the stove is plugged in. Even gas stoves need power.

➤ If the stove is getting gas and has power, clean the igniter near the burner or clean out the pilot light hole.

TERMINALS

Electric stove burner not heating?

The first thing Costas asks is, "Did you clean the stove recently?"
Usually the answer is yes, and the fix is easy. When you slid the burner
back into the top, the terminal didn't engage with the receptacle
under the stove top or the plastic terminal block got knocked out
of its holder. Lift the stove top to see what the problem is. The fix
usually involves reinstalling the terminal block. Also try spreading the
terminals slightly to create a tighter connection.

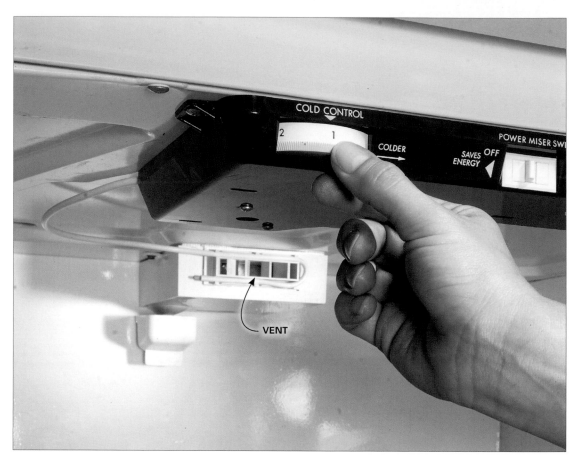

COLD CONTROL

2   1   COLDER →   SAVES ENERGY ◄ OFF   POWER MISER SW[...]

VENT

Check the temperature dial

Make sure the temperature control dial in your fridge or freezer hasn't been turned way down. Curious kids may have messed with it, someone may have bumped the knob or it's just set too low. Also make sure the vents in the fridge and freezer compartment aren't blocked by food containers—these vents supply the flow of frigid air.

RESET
BUTTON

Reset the disposer

All disposers have an overload feature that automatically shuts off the power when the motor becomes overloaded and gets too hot. Once the motor cools, simply push the reset button on the side of or under the unit.

Before you call an electrician

"I can diagnose about 30 percent of electrical problems over the phone. I play a game of '20 Questions' to see if I can avoid making a trip to the house."— Al Hildenbrand

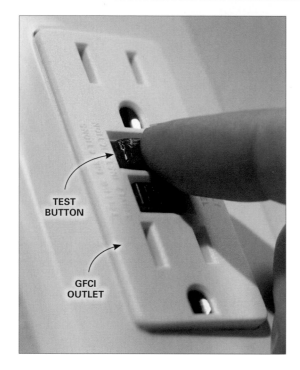

TEST
BUTTON

GFCI
OUTLET

Here are some of the most common complaints Al Hildenbrand gets, and the questions he asks.

"I screwed in a new fuse but I still don't have any power."

Are you sure you used the same amperage fuse as the one you replaced? Is the fuse good? Is it screwed in tight?

"I've checked the circuit breakers, but the outlet still doesn't work."

Some outlets are protected by upstream GFCIs or GFCI circuit breakers. Look in the circuit box for a GFCI circuit breaker and in bathrooms, kitchens and laundry rooms for GFCI outlets. Test and reset them. This may solve your problem.

"I replaced the lightbulb but the light fixture still doesn't work."

Are you sure the new bulb is good? Try it in another light fixture and make sure it's screwed all the way in.

"This outlet used to work. Now it's dead."

Check all the switches in the room. One of them might control the outlet.

Check the outlet

If any electronic item suddenly won't turn on, don't immediately assume it's broken. Plug in a radio or a lamp to make sure the outlet is working.

Check the breaker

When a light goes out or a switch doesn't work, you should first check the main electrical panel for a tripped circuit breaker. Look for a breaker switch that's not in line with the others. That means it's tripped. Switch it to the off position and then back on.

Before you call about heat or air conditioning

"We always ask, 'Is the furnace switch turned on?' You'd be surprised how many times someone in the house accidentally switches the furnace off."— **Bob Schmahl**

Not getting enough heat?

Another common cause of cold rooms during heating season is a blocked cold air return. Be sure your couch or an area rug isn't covering a cold air return vent because this can slow the entry of heated air into the room.

And, always check the furnace filter. Bob Schmahl says, "When I ask people when's the last time you changed the furnace filter and they give me that deer-in-the-headlights stare, I know what the problem is."

Furnace quit?

If you live in an area with snow and have a furnace that vents out through the side wall, make sure the vent pipes aren't plugged with frost or snow. Plugged vents cause the furnace to shut off automatically. Once you've unplugged the vents, reset the furnace by switching off the power: Either turn off the switch located on or near the furnace, or flip the circuit breaker that controls the furnace. Wait a minute, then switch the power back on.

DIRTY FILTER

16x25x1

Too hot or too cold?

One of the most common causes of insufficient heat or cooled air is a plugged furnace filter. Change inexpensive woven fiberglass filters once a month or buy a better-quality pleated filter and change it every three months to avoid heating and cooling problems.

Before you call for a noisy garage door fix

When a garage door makes noise, it's usually just screaming for a bit of TLC. We'll show you some fixes to quiet down any garage door. And, if you have a tuck-under or attached garage, we'll show you how to reduce the vibrations and noise that transfer to the living space.

Test the noise level by opening the door after each fix and quit when things are quiet enough for you. Before you get started, go to a home center and pick up a garage door lubrication kit. You'll get all the lubricants you need for this job. Also pick up rollers if you need them for the tip on p. 254.

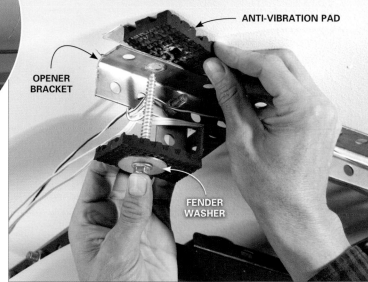

ANTI-VIBRATION PAD

OPENER BRACKET

FENDER WASHER

Isolate the opener

If you have an attached or tuck-under garage and your opener seems loud inside the house, try this step.

Mechanically isolate the opener from the garage rafters/trusses with rubber pads. Cut rubber pads out of an old tire or buy specially made rubber/cork anti-vibration pads. (Just search for "anti vibration pads.") You'll be adding about an inch in thickness, so you'll need four longer lag screws and four fender washers.

Add anti-vibration pads. Slide one anti-vibration pad between the mounting bracket and the ceiling and the second pad under the bracket. Then slip a fender washer onto the new lag screw and drive it into the rafter with a socket wrench or impact driver. Repeat on all four corners of the opener bracket.

Tighten the chain and lube the opener

A loose garage door opener chain makes loud slapping sounds and causes jerky door movements that smack the rollers against the track. So start by tightening the chain (find the procedure in your owner's manual).

If you have a track-drive opener, the next step is to lubricate the opener track with grease. If you have a screw-drive opener, grease the threads.

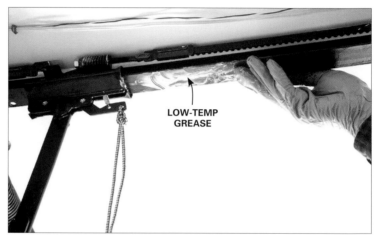

LOW-TEMP
GREASE

Grease the track. Squeeze a large dollop of grease onto your gloved hand and wipe it onto the track. Operate the opener several times to spread the grease along the track and into the trolley.

Lube the hardware

Next, quiet all the garage door's moving parts with garage door lube spray. It works much better than spray-on oils because it stays in place and dries to a greaselike consistency. The grease also does a better job of quieting moving parts. Repeat this step every six months.

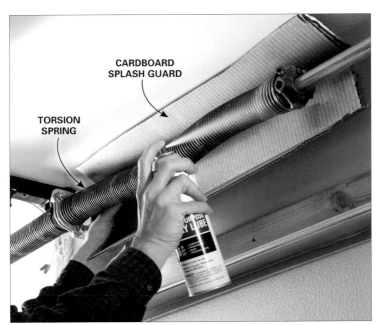

Lube everything that moves. Spray the roller shafts and hinges first. Wipe off the drippy excess. Then slip a piece of cardboard behind the torsion springs and soak them, too.

Install quieter rollers

If your garage door has steel track rollers, they're part of your noise problem. Buy eight "quiet" nylon rollers. They're equipped with bearings and cost a few bucks more than nylon "bearingless" rollers or nylon rollers without end caps, but they're quieter, roll smoother and last longer. You can find them at home centers and online.

Swap out the steel rollers for the new nylon ones (one at a time). **Caution:** If your door uses torsion springs mounted on the header above the door, do *not* attempt to replace the rollers in the two bottom brackets. Those brackets are under constant spring tension and can cause serious injury if you unbolt them. That's a job for a pro.

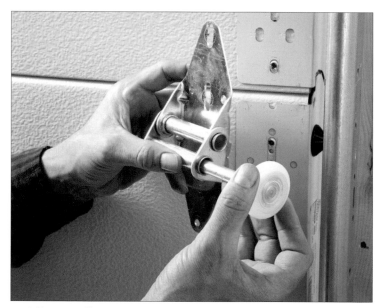

Install new rollers. Remove the hinge retaining nuts and tilt the hinge/bracket toward you. Swap out the rollers and reverse the procedure to reinstall. Then reinstall the nuts and snug them up with a wrench (but don't overtighten).